2 5 th A N N I V E R S A R Y

THE '85 BEARS

WE WERE THE GREATEST

Mike Ditka
with Rick Telander

TRIUMPH
B O O K S

This book is available in quantity at special discounts for your group or organization.
For further information contact:

Triumph Books
542 South Dearborn Street
Suite 750
Chicago, IL 60605
Phone: (312) 939-3330
Fax: (312) 663-3557
www.triumphbooks.com

Printed in the United States of America
ISBN: 978-1-60078-508-5

Content packaged by Mojo Media, Inc.
Joe Funk: Editor
Jason Hinman: Creative Director

All photographs courtesy of the *Chicago Tribune* except where otherwise noted

The game summaries, "Remembering '85" interviews, and statistical appendices appeared previously in *The '85 Bears: Still Chicago's Team,* copyright © 2005 by The Chicago Tribune. Used with permission. Portions of the main narrative text appeared previously in the book, *In Life, First You Kick Ass,* copyright © 2005 by Mike Ditka and Rick Telander.

*To those men on the field who made this all happen,
and to the memory of the Old Man.*
—M.D.

To the good life.
—R.T.

Acknowledgments

I want to thank all of those writers who documented the Bears' run to the Super Bowl, particularly the columnists and beat reporters for the *Chicago Sun-Times,* whose old news clips were so valuable in my research.

I also got insight and information from these books: *Halas by Halas,* by George Halas and Arthur Veysey; *Ditka: An Autobiography,* by Mike Ditka and Don Pierson; *Papa Bear,* by Jeff Davis; *It's Been A Pleasure: The Jim Finks Story,* by seven various writers; *Ditka* by Armen Keteyian; *Singletary on Singletary,* by Mike Singletary and Jerry Jenkins; and *McMahon,* by Jim McMahon and Bob Verdi.

—Rick Telander

Table of Contents

Introduction

To me, it seems like only yesterday that the Mike Ditka Bears ruled the earth. Part of that is because during the amazing and amusing 1985 season, I lived next door to the team. The east property line of my yard was the west end line for the Bears' practice facility in Lake Forest. A chain-link fence—with a number of large, rusty-edged, human-sized holes in it—a few ash trees, and some accidental buckthorn sprouts were all that separated my house from the gridiron.

My wife and I and our two baby girls had moved from a two-bedroom Evanston apartment in 1984, risking everything on a down payment and a strangling mortgage, heading farther north in the 'burbs where things were cheaper and we could afford—strange as it may seem now with current real estate prices in this area—our first house. The 100-yard grass field next door was vacant when we arrived in the spring of 1984. It was called Farwell Field, I learned, and belonged to Lake Forest College. Remarkably, the Bears shared the field all late summer and fall with the mighty Division III

Lake Forest Foresters, a band of cheerful, red-and-black-clad, nonscholarship collegians about the size of average high school players. The Foresters would tear up the field on Saturday afternoons against Beloit and Lawrence—really destroy the sod when they played in the occasional monsoon—and then the Bears would practice on the maimed surface the rest of the week. By late November the grass would be brown, clotted, and ruined. At the east end of the field was the low brick structure known as Halas Hall, with the large office window to the far south being that of young team president Michael McCaskey and the window to the north being that of young head coach Mike Ditka. In time I would realize that as I stood in our ground-floor bathroom when the leaves were gone, casually relieving myself, I could see into the working quarters of each man.

Of course, I didn't know much about this yet. I worked for *Sports Illustrated* at the time, and I loved sports. But mostly I traveled for my stories. To Washington and San Francisco and Pittsburgh, places where they had real NFL teams and real heroes. I had heard the Bears lived next door to our new place, but my mom had actually found the house and told me about it while my family was vacationing in Florida, and I made the earnest-money payment sight-unseen. At any rate, in May when our burgeoning troupe—soon to be six of us—moved our few possessions into the old house on Illinois Road, nobody was in the big yard next door.

Who cared about the Bears, anyway?

The year before they had finished 8–8. In 1982, a strike-shortened misfire, they had gone 3–6. The year before that, 6–10. The year before that, 7–9. You threw in with the Bears at your own risk. They hadn't won anything since 1963, three years before the Super Bowl was invented.

Still, the Bears had this fellow named Payton. And they had a nostalgia-laden tradition. And starting in 1982 they had a new coach with fire in his eyes, a sometimes-frightening, sometimes-inspiring former All-Pro tight end by the name of Mike Ditka. He had replaced Neill Armstrong, coming straight from a special teams job with the

Dallas Cowboys, apparently at old man George Halas's request. Which made folks wonder if the acerbic, grumpy Papa Bear had finally gone around the bend. Special teams coaches didn't become head coaches. Offensive coordinators did. Defensive coordinators did. Special teams coaches became not much of anything.

Ditka was a guy who broke racquets in rage when he played racquetball against Cowboys staff members like Dan Reeves and the great calm one himself, Tom Landry. Ditka made his Cowboys receivers run, and when they didn't run right, he swore at them. He challenged them to fight. Right there, on the spot! He turned red. He turned purple. As an athlete he had been overwhelming in high school, dominant at Pitt, ferocious in the NFL. In 1983, his second year as Bears head coach, he had been so infuriated after a loss, he punched a filing cabinet with his right hand, breaking a bone in the process. At the next game he inspired his team by saying, "Win one for Lefty." He was perpetually agitated, outspoken, a puffing volcano always on the verge of eruption. This was the head coach of the storied Chicago franchise, the granddaddy of the league? Help.

But, Ditka knew what it meant to be a Bear. For six years, starting in 1961, he had played like a maniac, on and off the field. He defined toughness and grit at the tight end position. Despite his Pennsylvania steel town roots and accent, he came to embody the soul of the black-and-blue division Bears along with two other striving souls—Gayle Sayers and Dick Butkus. Traded to the Eagles in 1967 and then to the Cowboys in 1969, Ditka played in two Super Bowls and was an assistant coach in two others. The idea of Ditka as a head coach seemed—what would you call it?—intriguing? What if his passion could be harnessed, focused, reproduced, and transferred like magic capes to all those players under him? What if…

Nah.

Gradually the Bears began to make their presence known next door. There was a minicamp or two. And sometimes I would see Ditka in a golf cart on the edge of the grass, observing, gesturing, sometimes seated with oddball young quarterback Jim McMahon or even with the great, squirming Walter Payton himself. Sometimes I could hear Ditka yell. Sometimes I could see his orange or blue sweatshirt glinting through the bushes as he limped from drill to drill. He chewed gum constantly, as though his jaw had to move nonstop to compensate for the uncertainty of his football-ravaged hip joints. There were the usual practice noises—grunts, whistles, hollerings, pads cracking, the leathery thud of punts departing Dave Finzer's and later Maury Buford's foot and the four- or five-second delay before a reciprocating thud was heard as each ball touched earth.

Sometimes I would stand next to the fence and watch wide receiver Willie Gault sprint effortlessly after seemingly far-overthrown passes from McMahon and gracefully pull them in. Sometimes I'd watch the boring recognition drills conducted for the defensive unit by the taciturn Buddy Ryan. At the end of certain practices the Bears would work on their two-minute drill— a loud, frantic blend of chaos and creativity that often ended with kicker Bob Thomas drilling a hurried field goal that would arch over the antique goalpost, soar above the chicken wire that hung uselessly from rusting poles above the fence, and bounce off the roof of my house.

Some of those balls the Bears managers were able to find. Some stayed in my yard for, well ... let's just say a few of them still haven't been returned.

I ran into Ditka a few times, sometimes after practices when I'd simply walk through a hole in the fence and have a chat with a player like Payton or Gary Fencik or, in years to come, new-draftee Jim Harbaugh. Indeed, it was Harbaugh who looked at my house and asked if I'd be willing to sell it. "Man, I could wake up, walk across the field, and be there for the meetings in two minutes," Harbaugh would say wistfully. I pondered a deal. Maybe I could gouge the first-round pick. But where would we move?

Like most writers, I didn't get too close to the head coach. Ditka was intimidating. He was in his mid-40s and except for the bad-hip, bad-foot hobble, looked like he could catch and crush the typical journalist with one paw. I have a photo of him holding my third baby, Robin, in his arms in 1988, tickling her under the chin, seated in the empty wooden bleachers next to the field. He was always civil enough, and always ready to sign autograph hounds' souvenirs, but he was...Ditka.

"We call him 'Sybil,'" Jim McMahon would write in his biography, *McMahon,* "after the girl in that movie. You know, the one who had all those different personalities? Mike will be calm one minute, then throw a clipboard the next. People don't understand that, but we do. The players figure he's just going from one stage to another. He's merely 'Sybilizing.'"

One summer a few years later workmen were at our house, adding a new bedroom and putting skylights in the two second-floor bathrooms. One of the carpenters was sitting on the exposed rafters of the open roof, looking down at the field and the practice session below. I knew he was a Bears fan, and I could hear him yell at Ditka—something about how stupid it was to trade away safety Dave Duerson. I heard muffled yelling, and then the carpenter came swinging down fast from his perch, looking terrified. What happened?

"Ditka yelled at me," he said, pale as drywall. What did he yell?

"'Use your hammer, not your mouth, jackass!'" While writing this book I took a break to see the soccer comedy movie, *Kicking and Screaming,* starring Will Ferrell and Robert Duvall as kiddie coaches and Ditka as—of course—himself. Enlisted by Ferrell as his assistant, the cigar-chomping Ditka screams on the first day to the assembled 10-year-olds: "I'm not just coaching soccer, I'M BUILDING MEN!"

This guy wasn't like Vince Lombardi or Landry or Chuck Noll or Joe Gibbs. Well, maybe there was a bit of Lombardi fury in him. But Ditka was unique. Unlike many high-profile coaches, he had been a great player. He was high-strung and ornery, unpredictable as a weather vane, and no one had ever considered him a brilliant tactician. But then, his actions were so loud and dramatic nobody much looked at his tactics. He had made so many impetuous mistakes in his life—in judgment, in execution, in choice—that he seemed to be constantly recreating himself out of penance or disgust or boredom into a new, more considerate, more actualized form of human. But through it all he pretty much stayed the same, and he always seemed able to grin at himself.

In his 1992 book, *Monster of the Midway,*

Armen Keteyian wrote that Ditka "is some sort of cultural aberration—at once the best and worst his town [Chicago] has produced." It is true Ditka has always carried the positives and the negatives of intense desire with him like twin briefcases, one in each hand. But if he seemed dangerous and threatening long ago, time has softened those ridges. He now is, without argument, Mr. Bear. He has pointedly stayed in Chicago after his football career. (Unlike, for instance, Butkus.) Please forget that brief nonsense down there as the New Orleans Saints head coach. (Lord, who else but Ditka would pose for a magazine cover as the groom in a wedding photo with Saints bride/tailback Ricky Williams?)

Ditka has a looming presence that shocks people who stumble into his path. No one could possibly mistake him for anyone but who he is. That head, that brow, those eyes, that walk, that mustache.

Twenty-five years have gone by since the Chicago Bears won the Super Bowl. In 1984, my first year in the neighborhood, they showed promise. They beat the evil Los Angeles Raiders for one thing, and they finished a surprising 10–6. They even won a playoff game, the first Bears team to do so in more than two decades.

Then in 1985, not only did they make it to Super Bowl XX, they snatched the champion's mantle and toyed with it and danced on its fabric like maniacs. It was Ditka's pinnacle. It was his fulfilled team. At its crescendo, that 1985 squad was, almost without question, the best NFL team ever. And it was the first to have larger-than-life characters sprinkled throughout. Quasi-nutcases, some. Or maybe it was just the first to have the media appreciate those characters, dissect them, revel in them, despise them, adore them—starting with the head coach. It was a sitcom played out for our entertainment.

I was next door during all of it—except when I was on the road observing the team—stunned like everyone else. To sit down two and a half decades later and have the man himself reflect on the journey has been entertaining, to say the least. We did most of the tapings in Ditka's own restaurant on—where else—Mike Ditka Way, in downtown Chicago. Some we did in the lounge at Bob-o-Link Golf Club in Highland Park, Ditka's home away from home. The tapes are littered with nightclub noises, plates crashing, vacuum cleaners roaring, toasts being proposed, the voices of autograph hounds, singing by impassioned Sinatra devotee John Vincent, wild laughter, shrieking, horrible jokes, pointless digressions, Ditka occasionally bellowing above the din, "Knock it off!" and they are, as you might guess, remarkable.

I couldn't bring Da Coach live to everybody's doorstep. But I captured his thoughts on that classic journey of yore, the one that seems so recent yet recedes daily like a plume of blue cigar smoke over an old oaken bar.

Bon voyage!

—*Rick Telander, July 2010*

chapter I

Where Are the Trucks?

The crowd was huge, half a million strong, and the plumes of condensed breath that came from the multitude of cheering mouths dissipated instantly in the stiff breeze. It was January 27, 1986, and downtown Chicago was frozen like a block of dry ice. The temperature was 8 degrees, with a windchill of 25 below zero. But the adoring masses were out to greet the returning heroes, direct from New Orleans, weather be damned. People barked like rabid dogs. They pounded their mittened hands in joy.

Less than 24 hours earlier the Bears had destroyed the New England Patriots in the Superdome 46–10, the largest margin of victory in any Super Bowl to that date. It wasn't a whipping; it was a humiliation. Consider, for instance, that starting Pats quarterback Tony Eason played all the way into the third quarter yet did not complete a pass.

"If I could crawl out of here," said Patriots linebacker Steve Nelson after the final whistle, "I would."

And the long-starved city of Chicago loved it. Bully for the bullies! On this manic Monday, Mike Ditka rose up through the sunroof of the limousine carrying him in the now-halted victory parade along LaSalle Street. There were hands to shake, supplicants to bless. His army of pilgrims was there, smiling and begging.

I stood up and, believe me, I wasn't hanging out there long. I was in a coat and tie and shades, and it was colder than frozen snot. I'd slept a little the night before, but not a whole lot. There was champagne that had to be drunk, and there was a team party. I did some TV show first thing in New Orleans when I got up—can't remember, *Good Morning America* or *The Today Show* or something—and then we got on the plane and they're the Smiths." I didn't mean anything negative about race or nationality or any of that stuff. It's that we represented Chicago, a work-ethic place. It's just a name I pulled up. A Polish name. It could have been Jim Grabowski, it could have been Tom Grabowski. Hell, it could have been Tinker Bell Grabowski. It symbolized that we were the hard-hat guys. The other guys ride in limos. We ride in trucks.

"See, Grabowski is the name I came up with for the players on our team, and it fit Chicago." —Ditka

there we were. All those people, and it was really, really cold. It was impressive. It would have been impressive if it had been 80 degrees out, but 25 below? It showed what our team meant to the city of Chicago. To all the Grabowskis.

See, Grabowski is the name I came up with for the players on our team, and it fit Chicago. I grew up in Aliquippa, Pennsylvania, a work-ethic community, where guys went to work with their lunch buckets, did their jobs, and came home with empty lunch buckets. So when we got ready for that second playoff game against the Los Angeles Rams, I said, "We're the Grabowskis,

Of course, there I was in a limo. But like I said, I was freezing my butt off, or at least the part of my body sticking out of the roof. We were all supposed to be in limos, 34 of them, but it was so cold that day, even with the sun shining bright, that most of the players were told to stay in the buses. I don't think they minded.

Some of the guys, like Super Bowl MVP Richard Dent, weren't with us. They were already flying to the Pro Bowl in Hawaii. But I knew what Dent had said the night before: "If we're not one of the best teams of all time, I'd like to see the others."

Yeah, that got right to it. We finished 18–1.

Fourteen times we held opponents to 10 points or less. We led the league in takeaways, yards given up, all kinds of stuff. Hell, 24 Bears players scored.

Me, I couldn't believe where I was. Mr. Halas had given me a chance. I don't think anybody else would have. There were people right in the Bears organization who didn't want me there, who thought I was the stupidest hire of all time. But Papa Bear had the say-so—he started the NFL!—and he gave me the job. I desperately wished he hadn't died two years before, so he could see me, see how I and the team had repaid him for his trust. Because this really was about a team, a group of guys who were kind of misfits who all fit together for that one time.

But, man, the cold! It was crazy.

And there I was, a Grabowski in a limo. ■

Bears coaches Johnny Roland, Ed Hughes, and Mike Ditka at work during win No. 1 against Tampa Bay.

Chicago 38, Tampa Bay 28
Balky Beginning Turns Out Well

A season of history began like anything but, with the underappreciated Bears offense bailing out the defense against what most considered a mediocre NFC Central opponent.

The Soldier Field crowd's expectations had been raised by a strong 10–6 season in 1984 followed by a playoff victory over Washington. But the Bears fell behind 28–17 at halftime as the Tampa Bay Buccaneers, not the Bears, were the smashmouth team at the outset.

When it was over, Tampa Bay quarterback Steve DeBerg had thrown for three touchdowns to Jim McMahon's two, and Bucs running back James Wilder had outrushed Walter Payton 166 yards to 120. Wilder ran wild through a Buddy Ryan defense that was still feeling its way without

Pro Bowl safety Todd Bell and defensive end Al Harris, both mired in contract impasses that would keep them out all season.

The Bucs scored first on a 1-yard pass to Calvin Magee, which the Bears answered with a 21-yard scoring pass from McMahon to Dennis McKinnon. But Kevin House scored from 44 yards out on another DeBerg pass. No one knew it then, but the Bucs would be the only team to score two first-quarter touchdowns against the Bears all season.

Jerry Bell gave the Bucs a 21–7 lead early in the second quarter on DeBerg's third scoring pass before a 1-yard McMahon run and a 38-yard Kevin Butler field goal brought the Bears within 21–17. However, Wilder powered into the end zone from 3 yards out for a 28–17 Tampa Bay lead at halftime.

Matt Suhey celebrates his third-quarter touchdown with Jay Hilgenberg and Dennis McKinnon.

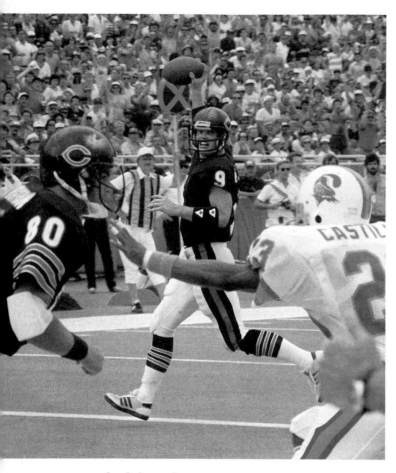

to his outside, into the path of the throw.

Dent deflected the pass, Frazier intercepted, and the result was a 29-yard interception return for a touchdown that ignited the Bears. The TD brought them back within 28-24 and shifted all the momentum to them.

They took the lead for good when Matt Suhey made a diving catch of a McMahon pass for a 9-yard score and sealed it when Shaun Gayle blocked a punt to set up a 1-yard McMahon plunge for the final touchdown. ■

Chicago 38, Tampa Bay 28
SEPT. 8, 1985, AT SOLDIER FIELD

BOTTOM LINE
21-point 2nd-half rally rescues season opener

KEY PLAY Leslie Frazier's 29-yard interception return for a touchdown at the start of the third quarter. It trimmed Tampa Bay's lead to 28–24 and sparked the comeback.

KEY STAT The Bears gained 436 total yards, their second-best showing all season.

The defense then came to life and struck with what head coach Mike Ditka and others considered perhaps the most important play of the season.

Twenty-two seconds into the second half, cornerback Leslie Frazier read DeBerg's quick three-step drop and broke before the sideline pass was thrown. At the same time, defensive end Richard Dent detected signs of the play and drifted

Jim McMahon strolls in for one of his two touchdowns (above), and safety and Dave Duerson drops in on Buccaneers running back James Wilder during the Bears' opening victory (right).

JIM McMAHON

No. 9, quarterback

"I t amazes me that we didn't win four of them. We lost 11 games in four years and only won one Super Bowl."

"I haven't watched a game in years. I was a player, that's it."

"Like I told Ditka years ago, 'I don't care what you call, I just want the freedom when I get to the line of scrimmage, if it's not a good play, to get out of it.' That's what these guys don't do now. Nobody wants to take it on their shoulders to say, 'I'm not going to call that play. It's not going to work.' They can just go in the locker room after the game and go, 'Well, the coach called it.' They don't want to take any heat. That's another reason I don't watch it. A bunch of robots."

"We had our moments. [Ditka] was a tough coach. Had we played together, I think he would've understood me a little bit better, had he been in my huddle. I think he finally figured out that I

"I thought the best player I ever played against was Wilber Marshall, and that was every day in practice until he went to the Redskins."

"I think the people who meet me and spend some time with me know that I'm not the guy they see in the papers."

"The fans [in Green Bay and Chicago] are about the same—maybe a little more rabid in Green Bay, because there's nothing else to do, other than icefish, and I didn't do that."

"Bears fans always treated me well, even when I came back in a Green Bay Packers uniform. I got cheered. That's why I kept living in Chicago."

"Played with a lot of great people. That's what I remember—guys I played with, friends I made in the league. I just had a good time." ∎

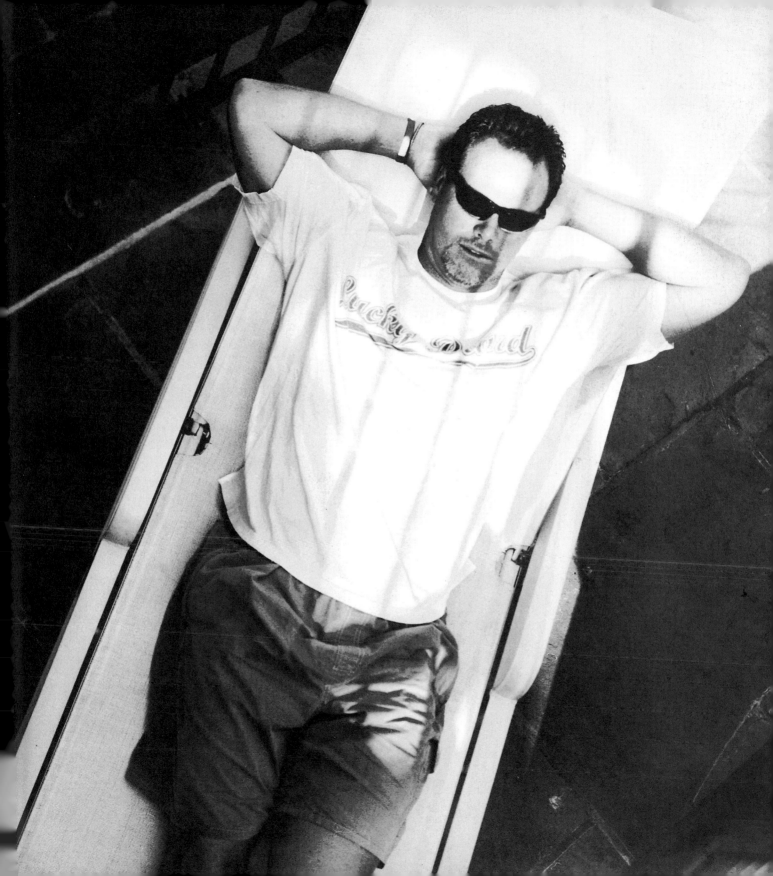

chapter II
We'll Be Back!

Mike Singletary stood in back of the team bench at Candlestick Park, facing not the debacle being completed on the field behind him, but the jeering, sneering San Francisco fans.

"Nice game!" hostile voices screamed. A lot of them sounded very drunk. *"The Bears suck!"*

Singletary's nostrils were flared, and his glinting samurai eyes were wide and focused. He was breathing hard. The clock was running out on this NFC championship game between the Bears and the 49ers, and the Bears were being dissected 23–0. It was January 5, 1985, and Chicago's high hopes for its 1984 team were being crushed. No Super Bowl here. Maybe none ever.

"We'll be back!" Singletary, the Bears' Pro Bowl middle linebacker, yelled in a fevered Southern minister's voice, facing the enemy. *"We'll be back! I guarantee you. We WILL be back!"*

"He was our quarterback, our first-round pick in 1982, my first year. He was smaller than most quarterbacks, and he wasn't in great shape and he was feisty. And he was different." —Ditka on Jim McMahon

The crowd hooted and pelted Singletary with more verbal abuse. On the bench Walter Payton had sunken so low into himself it appeared he was shrinking. He may have been crying. He had carried the ball 22 times for 92 yards, and they were hard yards. On one barely successful fourth-and-one run he had to break three tackles—in his own backfield.

The Bears' offense was impotent. It had totaled but 186 net yards to the 49ers' 387. And of course, it couldn't score. The loss was complete, overwhelming, destructive. And humiliating. San Francisco coach Bill Walsh had briefly used a 280-pound guard, Guy McIntyre, in his backfield as a flattener. It wasn't illegal. In fact, it was semibrilliant. But it hurt.

The Bears thought they had a stellar defense, based on the hyper-aggressive "46" scheme. But 49ers quarterback Joe Montana had whipped it by taking three-step drops and throwing in less than two seconds. San Francisco receivers Freddie Solomon and Dwight Clark had 11 catches for 156 yards between them. Bears fill-in quarterback Steve Fuller passed for just 87 yards and was sacked an astounding nine times by a San Francisco defense that was more Bear-ish than the Bears.

Fans began pouring out of the stands before the clock had expired. It was going to get ugly. For the Bears. The refs called the game with two seconds remaining.

Even Singletary, eyes set in fury, ran for the exit.

My God, did we hurt. I don't think anybody can realize how much we hurt after that game. I take the blame for a lot of it, because I thought with our defense, all we'd have to do was stay close, run the ball, and our defense would give us a chance to win. That was wrong. I was wrong. We had to score points, be more aggressive.

I said at the time that we got a lot of lessons out there. In life, you either teach or you learn.

Gary Fencik Remembers '85

Losing the 1984 NFC Championship Game to San Francisco

"We were only down six-zip at halftime and that's not much. But we were fortunate not to be down by a lot more, because we didn't have our starting quarterback in the game. I don't remember why Jim was out, but he was. Steve Fuller was in. It wasn't his fault. It was just a demoralizing loss. But the better team won. I went to the Super Bowl two weeks after that at Stanford, and the 49ers beat the Dolphins bad. With Dan Marino.

"From the Bears players' perspective that NFC Championship Game loss was devastating. It was so emotionally draining, and then we had to fly all the way back to Chicago. We were on that plane and it seemed like forever and it was no fun. But I had seen that the 49ers were a really good team. We all did. I think we learned from that.

"Then Ditka came in from the very first day of the '85 season, saying, 'We have a goal. We're going to win this year!' And we just built on the emotion. We had been on such a high going into the 1984 post-season, and then that loss was tough to accept. We didn't want that to happen again."

Professor or student. I hoped we learned. I was outsmarted by Bill Walsh, their great coach. And I was embarrassed. But we had a couple things going against us, too. Things that had nothing to do with the 49ers.

Our safety Todd Bell had played a great game against the Washington Redskins the week before in our first round, which helped get us into this game—and this NFC title game was as deep into the playoffs as any Bears team had been since the Super Bowl started. But against San Francisco, Bell had to replace our injured right cornerback Les Frazier, and second-year sub Dave Duerson replaced Bell. Later, Bell and Duerson switched positions. Our other safety, Gary Fencik, had a good game with two interceptions. But we were unsettled back there. Neither Todd nor Dave was a cornerback.

Also, we were without Jim McMahon. He was our quarterback, our first-round pick in 1982, my first year. He was smaller than most quarterbacks, and he wasn't in great shape and he was feisty. And he was different. What I was already finding out was that he was going to be injured a lot, because of the way he played. He played balls out, all the time. He had already suffered a lacerated kidney, which in a way was just par for the course. We'd had four quarterback changes in just that 1984 season because of Jim, but I didn't blame him.

I mean, there was no question that he shortened his career because of the way he played. He butted heads with linemen, he ran, he dove, he hung on to the ball too long. He played the way a linebacker plays the game. He had no regard for his body. But I couldn't change him. It would have ruined him. His persona was to put the pedal to the metal, and I kind

and he's got a beer in his hand and a six-pack under his arm. I think it was Miller, but it might have been something else. He has a wad of tobacco under his lip, too. First thing he says is, "I was getting dry on the way in."

I look at Finks, and he looks at me. Oh, brother. But it was okay—I played the game, and I did my share of messing around, and it wasn't

"I look at Finks, and he looks at me. Oh, brother. But it was okay—I played the game, and I did my share of messing around, and it wasn't going to kill him."

—Ditka on Jim McMahon

of liked that. But, man, the problems.

Fuller couldn't do anything in that NFC game, because we were playing catch-up most of the time, and they were laying for him. Steve was a great addition to our team, and tough as nails himself, but he wasn't McMahon.

Who was? I remember when McMahon first came to Chicago. We had just drafted him, and I was in the office with Jim Finks, the general manager at the time. McMahon walks into Halas Hall,

going to kill him. He had on a sport coat and slacks and sunglasses, of course. He had an eye that was damaged from when he was a kid—he accidentally stuck a fork in it or something—and he said he needed the shades for the pupil. Needed shades all the time. Fine.

After a while it was time for McMahon to talk to Halas. The Old Man was brutal. He'd only been with the team for 62 years. When I played, Halas did all the negotiations, all the contracts, everything. He was tougher than iron. He was mostly retired now, but he meets McMahon, and he looks at him and says, "You're not very big, you don't look very strong, your knees are lousy, you got a bad eye. I'm not going to pay you very much money."

McMahon looks at him, kind of curious. Maybe he yawned. He says, "I thought you drafted me."

Jim was something. Anyway, I knew we weren't bad enough to get shut out, 23-zip by the freaking 49ers. The guys knew it, too. In the locker room afterward I told them I'd take the blame for the mess. I thought we could shove the run at them. I thought we could bully them. I thought we were much more physical than they were. But I realized we would have to be creative and aggressive on offense next time, and we would have to score points.

Were we fighters or not?

And I couldn't forget how Walsh had this formation, and I looked in the backfield, and I'll be damned, there's a guard back there. That big old McIntyre. I said, "Okay. Good. Uh-huh." That stuck in my mind.

I'm talking to the team, and I tell them we will be back and we will play these guys again. I hadn't read it yet, but I know Walsh had a quote in the next day's paper where he said, "They have a great team. When they get their offense squared away with McMahon and get more experience with Fuller and the defensive backfield, I think next year they will be the team to beat."

That's fine. But I was mad as a sledgehammer. I had great respect for Bill. To a point.

I told the team, "We will beat these guys. You take care of the players next time, and I'll take care of the coach."

We had time to think about it. And fume. ■

Chicago 20, New England 7
Think This Is One-Sided?

It would be a preview of Super Bowl XX. The Bears' defense utterly dominated the Patriots' offense, holding New England to 27 rushing yards. The Patriots keyed to stop Walter Payton and eventually sent him out of the game with bruised ribs, but myriad other Bears did sufficient damage.

The Bears sacked Tony Eason six times—they would sack Eason and Steve Grogan seven times in the Super Bowl—and held the New England offense to 206 yards, 90 coming on a late touchdown pass from Eason to Craig James. They forced the Patriots to punt 11 times, the same number of rushes New England would try in the Super Bowl.

The Bears opened the game with a decisive 69-yard drive that needed only four plays before Jim McMahon hit Dennis McKinnon with a 32-yard touchdown pass. Kevin Butler made the halftime lead 10–0 with a 21-yard field goal on a day when the offense hammered the Patriots with 44 runs to only 23 passes after a 34-34 run/pass balance the week before. The defense was swarming, with Mike Singletary blitzing and picking up three sacks to go with an interception.

Matt Suhey scored on a 1-yard dive in the third quarter, followed by a Butler field goal from 28 yards. The shutout was lost on the Eason-to-James touchdown, but the Bears otherwise completely outplayed their guests.

In a precursor to a bit of '85 Bears history, McMahon was replaced by Steve Fuller late in the game. McMahon's back was acting up; it required traction in the days before and after the game.

Backup defensive end Tyrone Keys helps make life miserable for New England quarterback Tony Eason.

for much of the season would consider the defense's best game. New England had rushed for 206 yards in its season opener; it totaled 206 yards in this game. The Bears completed 13 of 23 passes for 209 yards to go with the 160 on the ground in another demonstration that while attention rightly was being paid to the defense, there was more to the offense than just Payton left and Payton right. ■

Chicago 20, New England 7
SEPT. 15, 1985, AT SOLDIER FIELD

BOTTOM LINE
A few months later, it would be worse

KEY PLAY
Dennis McKinnon's 32-yard reception from Jim McMahon 3:03 into the game. The TD gave the Bears a 7–0 lead in a game in which they were never threatened.

KEY STAT
The Bears held the Patriots to 27 yards rushing.

That would set the stage for the next Thursday in Minnesota, where McMahon was unable to start but came in to relieve Fuller with one of the legendary comeback performances of all time.

The Bears scored only one touchdown on four trips inside the New England 20. But for now they had to content themselves with what Buddy Ryan

Tight end Tim Wrightman racks up yards after catching one of his two passes against the Patriots (above). Otis Wilson, Dave Duerson, and Steve McMichael revel in a wicked hit on New England quarterback Tony Eason, who was sacked six times and threw three interceptions (right).

RON RIVERA

No. 59, linebacker

"**I** would love to be in a position [as a defensive coordinator] where people say, 'These guys remind me of the '85 team.' I would love to have that every day, every week."

"The one thing I loved about Mike Ditka is he was honest with you."

"One of the first things that happened to me in 1984 was Coach Ditka always made it a point that the rookies were introduced to Mrs. McCaskey, to Virginia, and she gave us the autobiography *Halas By Halas*. Ed, as ever, was joking, but I thought he was serious when he said, 'I hope you guys enjoy the book, and by the way there's going to be a test on this book.' So I read the book."

"Buddy Ryan was one of those guys that tore you down, broke you down, beat you up to build you up. He loved you and you learned to love him."

"Buddy said, 'You're slower than Buffone.' Once I found out who Doug Buffone was, I was really hurt."

"Guys were sniffling and crying [when Buddy Ryan told the defense he was leaving after the Super Bowl]. Real quiet. Then all of a sudden, out of nowhere, [Steve] McMichael goes, 'What a bunch of crybabies. We're getting ready to play the most important game of our lives, and all you guys can do is whine about this?' And he grabs a chair and throws it across the room, and it sticks in the chalkboard. If we'd have played them that night, we'd have beaten them 100–0."

"Walter Payton: As large an individual as he was in terms of the whole scope and magnitude of being an NFL player, he was a good person."

"I was telling a group of kids one time, 'Everybody talks about the money, the jewelry. That doesn't mean anything. What means something are the people in the room that you do these things with. That's what's special. Someday my son's going to inherit this [Super Bowl] ring, but it won't have the same value to him that it has to me."

"I was an Army brat. When I was growing up in the military, there was a rank system, a class system. There wasn't a black or white. When we moved back to the United States from Panama... I was stunned by the racism. I played flag football in junior high. We had a lot of black kids on our team, and one of the guys got cut, and this white kid from this small town looked and said, 'Y'all bleed red blood, too?' I was shocked. I guess I was naive." ■

chapter III

Rope Burns

Platteville, Wisconsin, is not near anything. Unless you consider Tennyson or Belmont or Arthur or Cuba City to be more than dots on a grand agricultural map. But that was the point. The dormant-in-the-summer University of Wisconsin-Platteville made the perfect spot for the Bears' training camp. Away from Chicago—five hours by car, unless you traveled at Payton speed and risked the almost-guaranteed speeding ticket—Platteville offered little but an insulated environment with lots of good flat football fields and meeting rooms and dorms far from prying eyes. Well, that wasn't entirely true. Members of the Chicago sports media would reluctantly make the trip—griping the whole way—and fans from southern Wisconsin and northwestern Illinois and eastern Iowa would pile into the family cars to make the hot summer trips to watch the Bears go through preseason camp.

But Platteville was a place for the Bears to come together and focus on the season ahead with relatively few distractions. In July 1985, that focus was keen and narrow. The coach was fired up. So were the veterans. Still, it wasn't as pleasant and unified an atmosphere as it could have been.

"Al was in between a linebacker and a defensive end; he was a slipper and a slider. You could put him up or you could put him down. Maybe he wasn't the fastest guy, but he was agile enough and he had a great wingspan." —Ditka on Al Harris

Two key defensive members of the Bears' 1984 team were holding out, looking for better contracts. Safety Todd Bell and linebacker/defensive end Al Harris did not report to Platteville with their mates. Singletary had been disgruntled over his salary, too, and was, at least in theory, a brief holdout. But the Bears restructured his contract, and he showed up on time. Harris and Bell, however, would not show up all year. It became one of the sad parts of the 1985 Bears' journey, a journey with so many epic overtones that would lead others to unique places—that two respected members of the stepping-stone unit would not be along for the ride.

And yet the band traveled onward, without the pair. Both Bell and Harris suffered from their exclusion, from the knowledge that business matters sometimes can't trump personal loss. Of the two, Bell took it the hardest.

There was tragic irony when, in mid-March 2005, Bell suffered a heart attack while driving his car in suburban Columbus, Ohio, crashing into a house. His death came the day after the Bears' Super Bowl players and coaches publicly agreed to work together with Bears management, often their enemy, on celebrating and capitalizing on the impending 20th-year anniversary of Super Bowl XX. The agreement was festively promoted in the Chicago media, with the Sun-Times *even running a color photo of alumni Otis Wilson, Dennis McKinnon, Steve McMichael, Dent, and Fencik grinning wide in front of a Super Bowl XX logo, festooned with the group's website: www.85worldchamps.com. Once again Bell had been reminded of what he had lost. Fellow holdout Harris told the* Chicago Tribune, *"Todd never let 1985 go. He felt betrayed. I had that feeling, too, but after a while, that's life."*

Todd Bell was 47.

I liked Todd a lot. But I never understood his holdout. Al's either. Todd had Howard Slusher as his agent, and that was Slusher's technique—sit out until you get what you want. Or don't play. I know players don't have much clout, but that was the biggest mistake of their careers.

Todd wanted something like $1.5 million for three years, and Jerry Vainisi, our GM, was offering a million. Al wanted, I don't know, maybe a hundred grand more a year than was offered. Todd was a hitter. He was a banger. In the Washington playoff game the season before he changed the tempo of the game. We only won 23–19, and he put a lick on their running back, Joe Washington, that was unbelievable.

Al was in between a linebacker and a defensive end; he was a slipper and a slider. You could put him up or you could put him down. Maybe he wasn't the fastest guy, but he was agile enough and he had a great wingspan. He used his weight well. And he was one of the nicest guys I'd ever been around, which just made it all so hard. But we had Duerson to replace Bell, and Wilbur Marshall had just finished his rookie year, and I knew he was going to be a star and could play where Harris was. If we moved Dan Hampton to defensive end from tackle and moved this huge new kid, William Perry, in next to Steve McMichael and did some

other things, we would be set to go.

Actually, when you got down to it, Todd was limited. He was a blitzer, a guy who could tackle really hard, but he had no coverage ability. He was almost like a linebacker. That was part of the deal with the "46" defense—it was named after old safety Doug Plank, No. 46, and Plank was just a big hitter, like Todd. I went in before camp to talk to Jerry Vainisi, and he said, "Mike, we're not gonna get these deals done with these two guys."

That was hard to take, but I thought about it, and I said, "We'll play without them." That might sound cocky on my part, but I thought we could replace them. And I wanted to reward the guys who were in camp and had been busting their asses. They'd done everything we asked, and I wasn't going to spit on them. You're with us or you're not.

I knew how the Bears were with money, how they'd always been. I came in as a rookie first-round pick in 1961 and got $12,000 and a $6,000 bonus. Then I went on to catch 56 passes for over 1,000 yards and 12 touchdowns and was named Rookie of the Year and made the Pro Bowl. The next year Halas tried to pay me less. You had to talk to the Old Man himself, face to face, in those deals. It was like looking at Mt. Rushmore. I finally got him all the way back up to $18,000,

"We had been building this team, and a lot of pieces were there before I came. The Bears were long known as a defensive team. But you had to have a quarterback, a good one. Otherwise we were never going to win." —Ditka

what I'd made the year before. But playing the game was the main thing; it always was.

Buddy Ryan was our defensive coordinator, and when I told him he wouldn't have Bell and Harris, he almost went nuts. Buddy was a holdover from when Neill Armstrong was head coach, as were most of the assistants. I know he thought Halas should have named him the next head coach, but there was nothing I could do about that. That didn't help the tension between us.

At any rate, I talked to Todd and Al through the years, and it was always a little sad. They both came back the next year, but it wasn't the same. They weren't starters, and they weren't going to be. That summer at the start of camp, though, I told our guys I believed in loyalty and I'd reward it. We were going to the Super Bowl because we had the players we needed.

Otis Wilson was there when I arrived in 1982, and so were Fencik and Walter and a lot of guys.

We drafted Mike Richardson and Marshall and Reggie Phillips and Jim Covert, whom I thought was the best pick I ever made, at left tackle. We had Keith Van Horne and Jay Hilgenberg and Mark Bortz and Tom Thayer on the O-line and McKinnon and Gault at receivers and Tim Wrightman and Emery Moorehead, who gave me so much, at tight end, and we had Maury Buford as our new punter and Kevin Butler as the kicker.

We had Mike Singletary in the middle on defense, a guy they'd tell you now was too small to play or some damn thing. Right. Because they don't measure your fricking heart! And, of course, we had Walter Payton in the middle on offense. He is to this day the greatest football player I've ever seen. Not the biggest. Not the fastest. Not the anything. Just the best player who ever played.

We had all kinds of people on that club, but they were focused like I was. Covert, I mean, on the first day he came to the Bears in 1983 I just

He was a military guy, remember. He never berated you, but he knew how to get you to do what was needed. It was plain old leadership, but deep inside it was cockiness— he knew that he could lead. —Ditka on Roger Staubach

said, "There's left tackle, That's yours." And he never let me down. He had a short career because he hurt his back, but what a warrior he was.

We had been building this team, and a lot of pieces were there before I came. The Bears were long known as a defensive team. But you had to have a quarterback, a good one. Otherwise we were never going to win. I remember all of the conversations Coach Halas and Jim Finks had about Vince Evans, who came in 1977, about what a great, great athlete he was. Yeah, he was a great athlete, but he wasn't a winner. Good or bad, that's just the way it was.

See, I played with a winner in Dallas, a guy named Staubach. I knew what it took to play the position and be great—hell, Roger Staubach's in the Hall of Fame. Maybe it took a cocky guy. Maybe not. You could have a calm guy like Roger, a guy who led by example, a guy who was smart, who you'd want in the foxhole with you. He was a military guy, remember. He never berated you, but

he knew how to get you to do what was needed. It was plain old leadership, but deep inside it was cockiness—he knew that he could lead.

Now, we took McMahon with the first pick when I had just gotten to the Bears, and he had a different kind of brashness. The one problem he had was with authority. He had a problem with his father, he had a problem with his Brigham Young coach, and he had a problem with me. Authority figures. He was defiant just because he didn't want to be known as a conformist or a guy who would listen. He sure as hell didn't care about being an All-American boy.

But his teammates, especially the offense, believed in him. I guess I had a problem a little like his. In 1982 Ed McCaskey, the chairman of the board, who was married to Virginia Halas, the Old Man's daughter, called me in. Ed and Virginia had a lot of kids, and their oldest son, Michael, was soon going to be president and CEO of the Bears. But Ed and Jim Finks wanted to talk to me about something or other I'd said in the paper. I came in and they both went at me, telling me I couldn't say whatever it was that I said. I honestly don't remember. And they're both dead.

But I do remember I told them, "Here's what I'm going to do. I'm going to leave here and go to my office and call Mr. Halas, and I'm going to ask who's running this football team." So I got him on the line and I said, "Mr. Halas, I have to know—who do I answer to, you or them?"

He said, "Kid, you only answer to me."

Maybe that wasn't an authority problem I had, but it was a control issue. And the thing is, Halas had been tough with me and he gave me crap after my very first game as head coach. It was at Detroit, and we lost 17–10. We had two different chances to score from the 1-yard line, and we didn't make it. The next morning I came into my office and there is the playbook opened to the page that says, "Quarterback Sneak." Man, was he ticked off!

Anyway, here we are in camp and we have to rally together, all of us. The ones who are here. The ones ready for this goal. McMahon may have been a jerk—I remember his first year he ran the mile and a half in almost 13 minutes, walking the last part, looking like he was going to puke and die, behind everybody but our very heavy offensive lineman Noah Jackson—but he was on board. I read that in 1984, even with his lacerated kidney, he'd gone out for Halloween with his teammates, dressed as a priest, drunk. He had a Bible with him, and I guess when you opened it, there were photos of naked women inside. Well, this was football, not religion.

There in Platteville we came together, because there wasn't anyplace to go. We had a pig roast or something and the cornfields were all around. Some of the guys rode scooters everywhere, and I guess that was a little risky. One year Van Horne, a huge guy at six foot eight, ran into a rope across a sidewalk or something, and if he hadn't been so tall he might have been decapitated. As it was, he just got some nice rope burns on his biceps.

We knew we were a pretty good team in 1984. And in 1985 we knew we were better, even if we had issues. Screw the issues.

We were ready to kick ass. ∎

Chicago 33, Minnesota 24
McMahon's McMiracle

This was the game that most point to as the difference-maker, the game that may have saved a season and certainly made the legend of Jim McMahon.

The Bears went into Minnesota with both division rivals sitting at 2–0. And for the second time in three games, the Bears would need a rescue.

It did not figure to come from McMahon.

The quarterback had spent two nights in traction for his back problems and was suffering from a leg infection. He didn't practice in the short week leading up to the Thursday night game, and, despite McMahon's insistence that he would play, Mike Ditka had rules to the contrary.

McMahon had been injured late in the 1984 season and hadn't played in the Bears' playoff games against Washington or San Francisco. So in games of this magnitude, he remained an unknown commodity.

All that changed midway through the third quarter. With 7:32 to play and the Bears trailing 17–9, McMahon was in Ditka's ear along the sideline and finally persuaded the coach to send him in to replace Steve Fuller, who had simply been unable to spark a team that was being outplayed on both sides of the ball.

The Bears had taken leads in the first and second quarters with Kevin Butler field goals, but Minnesota went ahead 10–6 at halftime on a 14-yard pass from Tommy Kramer to Anthony Carter. Butler kicked a third field goal, but another Kramer TD pass boosted Minnesota to a 17–9 lead.

Jim McMahon can exhale after Kevin Butler's fourth field goal gives the Bears their final margin.

AP Images

Still, the Vikings got up off the canvas with a 57-yard touchdown pass from Kramer to Carter, bringing them within reach at 30–24. But Butler finished the scoring with a 31-yard field goal.

Overshadowed by McMahon's pyrotechnics were 127 rushing yards for the Bears and five turnovers forced by the defense. But the Bears had shown the nation emphatically that they were capable of being a quick-strike team as well as the NFL's dominant rushing offense behind Walter Payton. ■

Chicago 33, Minnesota 24
SEPT. 19, 1985, AT THE METRODOME

BOTTOM LINE
His effort off bench is one to remember

KEY PLAY
Jim McMahon's three touchdown passes in a span of 6:40 in the third quarter.

KEY STAT
Most productive games in the careers of Willie Gault, who caught six passes for 146 yards, and Dennis McKinnon, who caught four for 133.

Enter McMahon. First play: McMahon pass to Willie Gault, 70 yards, touchdown. Second play: McMahon pass to Dennis McKinnon, 25 yards, touchdown. Before he was done, McMahon had completed 8 of 15 passes for a staggering 236 yards, including 43 on another touchdown pass to McKinnon, who accounted for 133 receiving yards.

Walter Payton led the Bears' rushing attack against the Vikings.

Chicago Bears quarterback Steve Fuller (4) is brought down by Minnesota Vikings cornerback Willie Teal after picking up three yards on a carry in the first quarter on September 19, 1985.

GARY FENCIK
No. 45, safety

"Ditka said that if we ever won the Super Bowl, people would remember you forever. I guess we're in the forever stage."

"I remember the first time we met Mike in an off-season camp in Phoenix. He basically told us for the first time—and this was my third head coach with the Bears—that our goal wasn't just to get to the Super Bowl, but it was to win it. But he said that 'half of you won't be there when we get there.' If you look at the roster, there was a two-thirds turnover from the time he gave that speech to the time we won it."

"I give Mike a lot of credit because who today would come in as a head coach inheriting a defensive coordinator who was hired by the president/founder of the club? That was a delicate situation. I don't think Buddy [Ryan] did anything to make that easier."

"I'm a huge fan of Buddy's. It was an honor to play in that defense."

"People always talk about how coaches discipline teams. Great teams discipline themselves."

"Walter Payton was such a leader that if you had people who came in and thought they were the next big thing, not that Walter said anything, but just by the way he conducted himself, I think he humbled you into appreciating what he did."

"I think of the great moments being beating Dallas 44–0, which for me was the first time that I had ever beaten the Cowboys in any preseason, regular season, or postseason game. I was in my 10th year."

"I felt pretty good coming off the field after New England's first field goal in Super Bowl XX, but there was something up on the scoreboard that basically said that 19 out of 20 teams that score first win. And I went from feeling pretty good to feeling like a Chicagoan. Growing up in Chicago, you can remember every good moment in sports because there have been so few."

"My dad was a basketball coach. I loved hoops. My mom attended all of my sporting events for myself and all of my brothers and sisters and knitted. So we had a lot of knitted sweaters when we were growing up."

———————

"My dad was an assistant principal of a high school, so I think that probably speaks for itself what the academic expectations were. I knew I wanted to enjoy football, but I was looking for something bigger, and Yale is a pretty impressive place when you visit it."

———————

"I'm really glad I went to business school at Northwestern. My first two classes were accounting and statistics, and we're coming back from beating the Raiders, and I'm studying for a final the next day, and everybody else is drinking beer and playing cards. I'm like, 'Why did I start business school during the football season?'"

———————

"A lot of people still continue to confuse Doug Plank and me. I had someone call me Doug Fencik. I don't even shake my head anymore. I just recognize the compliment."

———————

"Best piece of advice I ever got was: Make sure the door you go into has two doors going out." ■

chapter IV

No Saints Here

As the 1985 season approached, the Bears were evolving into a team with as much personality as football talent. It was a good thing Platteville was far away from major civilization, because there was a sense that Ditka's odd crew might not have withstood close scrutiny from discreet society or perhaps even the law.

Second Street was the name of the Platteville lane with the bars frequented by the Bears after hours. Players could do almost anything, according to Ditka rule, as long as they didn't get arrested or hurt. Pranks and acting crazy were fine, as long as nobody blew out a knee, ripped a hammy, broke a bone. There is a photo taken during spring practice before the team left for Platteville, and it shows the dynamic backfield tandem of fullback Matt Suhey and tailback Walter Payton getting set before a play. The interesting part is that Payton has the startled Suhey's gym shorts waistband in his hand, pulling it down low and back like a slingshot. Ditka didn't care. All he wanted was to win.

Platteville is Platteville, you know what I mean? The first couple years we'd played in Lake Forest, and there were too many kids and mothers and all that around. Hangers-on everywhere. I thought we could bond better up in the boondocks. I know the guys went out at night. They had fun, and that was okay. They weren't a bunch of saints. John Madden used to have a coaching philosophy that went like this: be on time, pay attention, and play like hell. And that pretty much sums it up. I know Van Horne almost killed himself on that scooter, but when I was playing, I remember we were running across a field trying to get away from the cops who were chasing us, and a couple of the guys tripped over wires strung between two posts and almost broke their legs in half. That's football. There's a time to play and a time to have fun. If it's all drudgery, I don't think you can win. I mean, these guys aren't wimps. They are who they are. Even a stoic guy

I can see that we were like a three-ring circus. There was something going on every day. I didn't read the papers back then, so I had no idea how nuts things were. But I know I tried to deflect some of the attention onto me, because I didn't want the players under any pressure except to go out and play. If the press thought I was an ass, fine. Didn't bother me. I was on a mission from the moment I took the job.

"Coach, who are you kidding? My philosophy is exactly the same as yours. My philosophy is to make the Bears something special, and to kick people's asses!"
—Ditka to George Halas

like Tom Landry, my coach when I was in Dallas, let guys have fun. Actually, he didn't know what guys were doing. He could have known, but he didn't want to know. That's a choice. That was "America's Team" with this clean-cut image. But the things guys were doing were off the charts. Still, we showed up every day, practiced our butts off, and played like hell on Sundays. That's what I wanted from my guys.

Looking back at all these clippings from 1985,

And the success could have happened sooner. I blew the first game I coached in 1982, up there in Detroit, by not scoring from the 1-yard line, twice! It made me feel bad, but it made Mr. Halas feel a hell of a lot worse. And I wanted to please him. I wanted him to know I was worthy and a Bear through and through.

My first week as coach I gathered everybody together and said, "This is going to be a good news-bad news announcement. The good news is we are going to win the Super Bowl. The bad news is a lot of you who don't care enough aren't going to be with us when it happens." I meant that. We had a lot of selfish guys back in 1982, but I knew the Fenciks and Paytons and Suheys and Hamptons would be with me.

See, George Halas embodied the Bears, and I wanted to embody them, too. Not many people know this, but in 1978 I wrote Mr. Halas a letter. I was the special teams coach for the Cowboys, and I was no big deal. Maybe I was a little wild. But what I said in the letter was, "We didn't part on the best of terms when you traded me, but I would love to come back some day, back to Chicago, and be the head coach. I'm not ready yet, but I will be some day. I'll bring back Chicago Bears tradition and pride. I promise."

Sid Luckman, the great old Bears quarterback, told me Halas always kept that letter. Sid and Mr. Halas were best friends. See, for me, it was the Bears only. I wanted nothing else. It was my ultimate goal. Just the Bears. That and winning the Super Bowl.

A few years went by, and then after the Cowboys lost to the 49ers in the 1981 playoffs, a really tough game where Dwight Clark made that great catch from Montana in the end zone, Coach Landry called me into his office.

"There's somebody who wants to talk to you," he said.

"Who?" I asked.

"George Halas of the Bears."

It excited the hell out of me. Tom gave me his blessing, and I got on a plane to Chicago. It was all cloak and dagger there, with Halas's right-hand man Max Swiatek, his driver and longtime helper, picking me up at the airport and taking me to Halas's place at the Edgewater Beach condos up on the north side near Lake Michigan. We sat at the kitchen table and he asked me some stuff. I was really keyed up, and I knew it wasn't him when he said, "What's your philosophy about football?"

"Coach, who are you kidding?" I said. "My philosophy is exactly the same as yours. My philosophy is to make the Bears something special, and to kick people's asses!"

He just nodded. He looked right at me. He said, "Okay, I'm going to give you a three-year contract to be our new head coach. One hundred thousand dollars a year. That's it."

I said, "No."

He was stunned. "What do you mean? You can't do it?"

"No," I said. "I will do it. But I have to have a 15 percent raise each year."

I thought I was really being cool. Hell, that would still make me one of the lowest-paid coaches in the league. But it didn't matter. It wasn't about money. Nobody else had offered me anything. It was just something to show I was my own man.

So he gave me the deal—$100,000, $115,000, $130,000—and we shook hands, signed the contract, and that was that. But what I really wanted was his respect. I meant it when I wrote that letter. I felt the Bears were my destiny. And George Halas was the Bears. His son Mugs Halas had died, and that left George's only other child, Virginia, and all her children as heirs to the family business.

But I knew deep inside he believed in me, the outsider, the old tight end. I think he believed that I was a lot like him. When he was lying in the hospital a year or so later, there were only two people he wanted to see—his secretary, Ruth, and me. Nobody else. I talked to him about the players we had just drafted. I told him he'd like Covert, that he was kind of similar to old-time star Joe Stydahar, and the Old Man liked that. He was very sick at that time, but he told Ruth to give me a special bottle of champagne he had. "Give this to Mike," he told her. "For when they win the Super Bowl."

It makes me sad because the bottle is out there on the wall, in a place of honor in my restaurant, and he wasn't alive when we opened it.

But I didn't know what was going to happen. I told the players they deserved to win it all, but nobody could foresee the future.

We came out for the opening game against the Tampa Bay Buccaneers and we felt we were in a good position. Platteville had been hot and tough, and Buddy had his defensive unit in good shape from all of the running they did. My guys, the offense, were ready to go, too, especially since McMahon was back for his first start since the kidney injury the previous November. I figured beer must have been part of his cure. Maybe it filtered out the bad stuff.

We were favored by a touchdown or so, partly because the Bucs were playing in Chicago, partly because our defense was so good, and partly because their star defender, Lee Roy Selmon, was out. We'd set the NFL sack record the year before, so everybody was sure our defense would dominate.

But it didn't. We gave up 28 points in the first two quarters, over 300 yards in the game, and were down 21–7 early and then 28–17 at the half. It was September 8, and it was hotter than blazes on our artificial turf at Soldier Field, something like 137 degrees at turf level. Maybe that's why the fans booed us when we came off at the half, because they were roasting. But I don't think so. We

Gary Fencik Remembers '85

Training Camp at Platteville, Wisconsin

"What a contrast Platteville was to the old days. Before Mike came in as coach we always practiced in Lake Forest, which was in the far north suburbs of Chicago, but still near the city. Going up to Wisconsin isolated the team from just about everything. It made the bonding more pleasurable.

"There we were in the middle of nowhere and we had bicycles and scooters to get around. It was funny seeing everybody zipping back and forth that way. Keith Van Horne is 6'7" or 6'8", and well, if he'd been a shorter guy he would have been decapitated when he ran into that chain or rope or whatever it was. Scooters weren't the smartest things for us to have, but we used them to get to town to have some beers after every practice.

"Training camps can be tough and hot, so the trainers had all these big tubs filled with ice water by the field. After practice guys would climb in. It sounds horrible, but, man, did it feel good. I always used them. I remember Fridge being in his tub and there wasn't much room left for the ice cubes.

"The worst part about Platteville was driving back through all that country to Chicago. The cops were just waiting to nail everybody."

weren't playing as a unit. This offensive and defensive split wasn't good. We had to be one.

Fortunately, McMahon was on target, and Payton was running the way he could. Walter carried the ball 17 times for 120 yards, and Jim completed 23 of 34 passes for 274 yards and two TDs. He also ran for two scores and didn't hurt his kidney in the process, for which I was thankful. It was nice the offense bailed out our defense for once. In fact, that helped us all, because, like I said, there was some tension between the two sides. And it was nice that McMahon got NFC Player of the Week honors for leading the charge. But it wasn't a game to be thrilled about. I was proud that our offense proved it could strike back. But we all knew we needed that D if we were going to go anywhere.

If we had lost that game, people would have said, "I told you so! You bums were nothing but a flash in the pan! San Francisco sucked you dry!'"

I thought back to the previous three years I'd been coaching the Bears. At the beginning we were losing all of these games we should have won. It worried me. But then we had Bob Avellini playing quarterback, and he was one of the biggest screw-ups I'd ever met. I had no idea what he'd do.

We're playing out in Seattle in 1984, and Avellini is starting because McMahon—guess what?—is already out with an injury. We're ahead, 7–0, Payton's averaging over five yards a carry, and it's second and 4, and we have a nice play called. Oh yeah, we're undefeated at the time— 3–0. Then I hear Ed Hughes, our offensive coordinator, standing next to me, say, "Oh, no."

"What, Ed?" I yell.

"The son of a bitch is audibleing!"

Avellini audibles to a hitch, from a fly pattern

He nods.

Then we're up in Green Bay the next year, and he does the same exact damn thing. I was purple. I was green. I was subhuman.

"That's it!" I screamed. "You're done!"

He looks at me and says, "Well, you never liked me anyway."

"Don't LIKE you?! You #%&*!@+!!%—!—"

I was going to kill him. Right there. Tear his

I was going to kill him. Right there. Tear his flesh off like a jackal. I was so mad my neck veins had veins. —Ditka on Bob Avellini

with max protection, and the Seattle cornerback picks the ball off on a dead run and he's going so fast in the other direction for a touchdown he nearly breaks his neck when he hits the end zone wall. Bob comes out of the game, which we went on to lose, 38–9, and I say—shit, I am trembling— "Bob, why would you do that, son?"

"Well, I thought—"

"Don't THINK!" I scream. "Please. Don't." Then I add, "Bob, if you ever do that again you will never—ever—EVER—play another down for me! DO YOU UNDERSTAND ME?"

flesh off like a jackal. I was so mad my neck veins had veins. Everybody was holding me back. I mean, he did the same thing!

Years later we were playing the Vikings up at that indoor roller rink they have in Minneapolis, and Jim Harbaugh was my quarterback. I said before the game, "It's gonna be loud out there. No audibles. Your linemen can't hear. I'm not going to put you in position to call a play that won't work. Okay? Got it?" Harbaugh nodded. Everybody nodded.

In the game we're beating the Vikings, 20–0, and I have a fly route to Gault called. Up the sideline. Harbaugh audibles to a hitch. Interception! We lose the game 21–20. There are photos that ran after that where I'm getting ready to strangle Harbaugh. I was wrong on the sideline, and I've calmed down through the years, and two wrongs don't make a right. BUT I DON'T UNDERSTAND WHEN PEOPLE DO THINGS LIKE THAT! Call the damn play!

Now the thing about McMahon was he was out there on his own, too, and he'd drive you crazy with audibles. But he could read a defense, he was a master at seeing the field, and he could sense the blitz.

So we had a chance with Jimmy Mac. Thing was, would the little turd survive? In 1984 he missed seven games plus the playoffs with everything from a hairline fracture of his hand to a bad back to that kidney thing.

In 1984 when we played the Raiders, it was about the most brutal game I'd ever seen. I told my players we had to beat them, it was the only way to get to the next level, to prove to ourselves we belonged. The Raiders knocked out Jim, could have killed him with that kidney injury. And we knocked out their quarterback. Guys were getting carried off the field left and right. I think the Raiders even had to put Ray Guy, their punter, in at quarterback. But we won 17–6 over the mighty Raiders. Our defense kicked ass. Our record was 7–3, but McMahon was done for the year, and we couldn't sustain. You gotta have a quarterback. I realized that.

McMahon was back now, and I prayed he would last. I know I was frothing at the mouth half of the time early in my career. He annoyed me so much—I swear he would wear stupid clothes or say crazy things on the sideline or to the press or grab the mike and blabber on the team plane or go out and get plastered, just to make me boil.

But I knew this. If you're going to be the bully, you have to beat the bully. And the bullies were everywhere.

And we needed this crazy quarterback. We were 1–0, just getting started. ■

Chicago 45, Washington 10
Electric Gault Lights a Charge

For most of the first quarter against Washington, the Bears looked like anything but the high-powered bunch that had blindsided the Vikings in the last game. They were outgained 141–2, and Walter Payton was on the way to a day that would give him 6 total yards on seven carries, one of the worst days of his career. They finished the afternoon with their fewest rushing yards, passing yards, and first downs of the season, and they heard a smattering of boos. Jim McMahon was 0-for-4 and threw an interception in the first quarter.

But they finished the day 4–0 after handing the Redskins their worst beating in nearly 25 years.

What happened was another turning-point play, again involving Willie Gault, as it had on the first McMahon miracle touchdown in Minnesota. With the Bears trailing 10–0 after a Mark Moseley field goal early in the second quarter, Gault took a Washington kickoff at his own 1-yard line and turned loose some of the legendary speed that made him a unique weapon for a unique team.

His touchdown sparked a 31-point blitz in the quarter as the defense completely shut down Joe Theismann's offense. After the Gault touchdown, the Redskins managed a total of one yard in their next three possessions, leaving the Bears with field position that set them up to score on drives of 14, 22, and 36 yards. McMahon passed to Dennis McKinnon 14 yards for a touchdown, followed that with a 10-yard TD pass to Emery Moorehead, then caught one of his own on a 13-yard heave from Payton.

Mike Richardson and Gary Fencik nail Art Monk, who coughs up the ball.

McMahon threw a third touchdown pass in the third quarter, finding Payton for a 33-yard score, and Dennis Gentry ended the scoring with a one-yard dive.

Washington had been a critical game in the 1984 playoffs, in which the Bears discovered and began to believe that they belonged on the same field with some of the NFL's best. Now they had gone a step further and confirmed that they were one of the NFL's best in their own right. ■

Chicago 45, Washington 10
SEPT. 29, 1985, AT SOLDIER FIELD

BOTTOM LINE
31-point 2nd quarter turns deficit into win

KEY PLAY
Willie Gault's 99-yard kickoff return for a touchdown. The play kick-started the Bears on a 31-point second-quarter outburst.

KEY STAT
The Bears scored on five consecutive possessions in the 2nd quarter.

What the game represented was the third time in four weeks that the Bears had rallied to win after trailing by more than seven points, and the result gave the Bears the NFL lead in scoring. The Redskins outgained them 376–250, but the Bears were beginning to dominate offensively as much with McMahon's passing as with Payton's running.

Jim McMahon grabs a touchdown pass from Walter Payton in the second quarter (above). Walter Payton, who gained only six yards rushing, bangs off a pair of defenders (right).

DAVE DUERSON
No. 22, safety

"**M**y dad is my hero. My dad's decorated—two Bronze Stars from World War II, fought in the 3rd Army Signal Corps directly under Patton. He spent a lot of his time behind enemy lines."

"So when I went to work for Buddy Ryan, it was like a joke. Buddy Ryan and Mike Ditka couldn't intimidate me. Buddy certainly had attitude, but his was self-serving. Very much so. You were either one of his guys, or you weren't. In my case, I wasn't."

"Buddy just absolutely hated my guts. Hated my guts. I called my dad when I first got drafted and I told him, 'Dad, I didn't graduate from college to go through this.' My dad believes that every male child should do two years in the armed services. I tell you that as a precursor. So he says to me, 'Well, it sounds to me like you're in the army.' So I said, 'OK, Dad, I'll talk to you later.' Short phone call."

"Every day Buddy would tell me he was waiting for me to screw up one time. So I played through that whole season with the defensive coordinator telling me that he was rooting for me to screw up so he could get Todd Bell back. So I became an All-Pro myself."

"I think [Patriots quarterback] Tony Eason knew [Super Bowl XX] was over the second series. Absolutely. He picked himself off the turf on each play of the first series and the second series. Their offensive line couldn't handle our guys. With all the things we were doing at the line of scrimmage, we were calling out their plays before they could execute them."

"I was projected to go to Parcells with the 10th pick in the first round. He took Terry Kinnard instead. I was talking about the importance of law school. It was never just football for me. It cost me two rounds in the draft."

"I think we should've won three Super Bowls. But they started shipping guys out." ∎

chapter V

Bodyslams and All-Day Suckers

The New England Patriots were coming to town. Coached by Raymond Berry, the Patriots had won their first game and had a fierce defense and a workable offense directed by third-year quarterback Tony Eason. Nobody knew that New England might figure into the Bears' journey somewhere else along the trail. For now all that mattered was keeping the dream alive, the quest.

One issue that popped up again during the week was the sometimes harmless but sometimes nasty rivalry between the Bears' offense and defense. A fight had broken out in practice midweek between offensive guard Mark Bortz and defensive tackle Steve McMichael. Actually, there had been two fights between the men. Fights can show intensity and desire. But they can also show pettiness and lack of respect. Ditka was a little worried about this last mini-brawl.

I guarantee you I never moved three feet when the fight happened between Bortz and McMichael, and I don't think Buddy moved, either. It wasn't that I wasn't concerned, but some things have to be settled without a lot of interference. And what could I do, anyway?

McMichael, that's just the way he was. He was a tough Texas boy, a free agent we picked up because he had tons of heart. He was a little out there at times. They said he wore his clothes in camp until he had a pile of dirty stuff, then he'd just turn the pile over and wear it all again. One of his hobbies was rattlesnake hunting. But he would get in your face and never shy away from anything. I love Steve McMichael. Bortz was quiet, a six-foot-six, 270-pound guy from a little town in Wisconsin, who had been a defensive player and co-captain at Iowa. He was a defensive lineman before he switched to offense in the NFL, so maybe that had the two of them going a little bit.

One problem we had was we were always going against our own defense in practice, and sometimes they were so fired up that we couldn't get a damn thing accomplished. I'd yell at Buddy, "For Chrissake, we're not playing the Bears next week!" But there was tension—football is a mean game—and those defensive players had great chemistry and great pride. Buddy had them cranked up like assassins. They'd run that "46," and it was like there were 50 killers on the line ready to slit your throat.

But then—and I think it may have been a week or so after we had bailed out the defense against Tampa Bay—we finally got the defense's respect. The exact date of a lot of these things gets blurry. It wasn't like I was keeping a diary, and after coaching the Bears for 11 years, I may get some things jumbled. But you don't forget the moments that jump out at you, the ones that changed things. At any rate, we were at practice, no media was around, and McMichael was mouthing off to the offensive line. Who knows who he was pissed at. But Jim Covert just grabbed him and body-slammed him. Now I love Steve, as I've said. He never complained about

anything, fought through any pain he had. And he was a tough guy. But Covert was a high school wrestler in Pennsylvania who had pinned all but one of his opponents his senior year. He was quick and agile. He was one of the quietest guys on the team. He'd been an English major in college. He'd gone to Pitt, my old school, and he was best friends with Danny Marino. But he could be pushed only so far, and you did not want to mess with him.

He slammed McMichael, who would go on to be a pro wrestler—one of those guys hitting other guys over the head with folding chairs and briefcases—and it showed the defense we weren't taking any more shit off them. It ended as quickly as it began. There was silence for a bit, and then I blew the whistle and said, "Let's get back to practice." You'd be surprised how much that ended the crap.

I coached the offense. Buddy had the defense. That's just the way it was. But a team doesn't have two sides, it has one. And the respect has to go back and forth, between everybody. McMichael made our guys better by the way he practiced. Nobody liked it at times. It wasn't a picnic out there. It was not a walk in the park. We were in pads every day up until Saturday.

The point is we had an offense that controlled the ball for a reason. We knew that if we gave our defense enough time to rest, they could go out and be animals. Who gives a damn if you won 40 to 30 or 10 to nothing? Actually, I like 10 to nothing. So our offense led the league in first downs and time of possession by design. We needed respect. Just as our defense already had respect.

Buddy was tough on his guys. He ran them, had them do ladder drills, ups-and-downs, and there were times when I'd have to tell him to stop. My offense was conditioned, too, but like with the receivers, they ran their asses off all practice long, so what was the point of running them at the end? But Buddy believed in those whistle drills for his guys. They hated them, but they never, ever quit, because they knew the reason for doing them. The defensive guys were as tough at the end of games as they were on the opening series. They were in shape. Buddy had their total attention and total respect.

As a coach, it was never about me. I had a bad temper and I got crazed at times, but what I wanted was to win. And when a team wins, everybody wins. It's about challenging the other team, doing everything you can with every bone in your body, because losing is rotten. When I got traded from the Eagles to the Cowboys, I went from being a pretty good individual player to being a team player, because I realized my value was not in catching 60 passes a year—they had guys to do that. What they needed from me was to angle block, pass block, take out linebackers for the runners behind me like Calvin Hill or Duane Thomas or Walt Garrison or Dan Reeves, whoever was carrying the ball. I understood how important I was to the team, not how important I was to myself. That Super Bowl championship ring the Cowboys won in 1971, when we beat Miami 24–3, sure felt good on my finger.

I suppose, right from the get go, teamwork and foresight by other people were part of my pro career. In college I'd played both ways, and the teams that wanted me—Washington, Pittsburgh, and San Francisco—were going to make me play linebacker. But the Bears took me, and the Old Man said, "You're a tight end." Did anyone know what a tight end was back then? Not really.

The whole idea of a big guy in close catching a lot of passes was kind of new. We played the Eagles in 1961, and a linebacker named Chuck Weber grabbed me and threw me down. He lined up right over me and forced me outside, and I couldn't do anything, and then he'd force me in, and the middle linebacker would knock me on my ass. Sometimes both of them would pound me, hold me down. I told Halas, "Those guys are holding me, Coach! Pushing me in, out—I can't do anything."

He and Luke Johnsos—the wide receivers coach, but really the offensive coordinator, even though we didn't have those titles back then— discussed this, and then Halas said to me, "Flex out two to five yards. Put the outside guy on an island. See what he does with that."

So I flex out on some of the pass plays and some of the runs, almost like a slot. What happens when I run a slant now? If I'm blocking the linebacker on a run, he's already out of the play. He's not gonna be a factor. We did it, and it worked. I mean why run through someone when you can run around them? Well, okay, sometimes you just gotta knock the crap out of a guy, because it is football, and kicking ass is fun. But how many great players are you going to intimidate?

You think you could intimidate Chuck Bednarik? Hah! Break his arm off and he'd throw it at you. How are you going to intimidate Ronnie Lott? Or Dan Hampton? Or Mike Singletary or Walter Payton? You might beat them, but you're not going to intimidate them, not because they're scared of what you're doing. Hell no. You beat the yolk out of people. But you outsmart them, too.

I had run-ins with guys like the Packers' Ray Nitschke, that bald guy who tried to tear my head off constantly. I had run-ins with a lot of great players. I hit them high, I hit them low—and they hit me that way, too. Bill Pellington, the Colts' linebacker, was wearing my ass out one game. He was slugging me, and I was slugging him. And finally I ended up with this cloth thing on my arm with a hunk of lead at the end, like a freaking weapon. I ran to the official and said, "That sshole's trying to kill me with a chunk of lead!"

The ref grabbed it out of my hand and said, "Gimme that, you idiot. It's my flag!" He threw it at us and it hit my arm. I was so embarrassed.

Pellington looked at me and said, "Ditka, I don't need lead to beat your sorry ass!"

Anyway, the Patriots game—Game 2 of the regular season—begins and our defense is back to what it should be, an attacking force. The offense had come from behind in the Tampa Bay game to win that one, and now the defense is returning the favor.

They're going after Eason and the Patriots runners like they're free beer. It was kind of funny,

because on Friday I happened to see this stupid-ass thing called the Dunkel Rating in a newspaper that was lying open. I also saw that our defense was ranked 23rd against the rush, even though it had led the league in rushing defense the year before. One game. Fricking statistics! And this Dunkel thing had the Bears rated only 12th best out of the 28 NFL teams. Fine. Screw 'em all. Dumb-Ass Rating is more like it. We'll see how it ends.

McMahon started off the game with a 32-yard touchdown pass to Dennis McKinnon, who was still battling back from off-season knee surgery. Dennis was a skinny guy, but like the guys I loved on this team, just tough and nasty, and he'd give you everything he had. That 7–0 lead was all we needed. New England couldn't do a thing against our defense. They had 27 yards rushing, and Eason got sacked half a dozen times and threw three interceptions. They wouldn't have scored at all except for a mistake on coverage when fullback Craig James caught a little pass across the middle and outran Wilbur Marshall for a 90-yard score in the fourth quarter. We were up 20–0 before that, and we won 20–7. Take away that pass and they only had 116 net yards. We had 369.

What I liked was the Patriots had six sacks the week before, and they got none against us. Our offensive line of Tom Thayer, Jay Hilgenberg, Keith Van Horne, Jimbo Covert, and Mark Bortz was developing into a cohesive unit. It's so important to have that communication and camaraderie when blocking, the same guys lining up together day after day, knowing each other's traits and techniques and personalities. We had that working now.

The Patriots keyed all game long on Payton, who was a little beaten up going in, and he only gained 39 yards. No problem. That opened up other things, including 37 yards rushing for backup Thomas Sanders and a TD run for Suhey. We also got two field goals from our rookie kicker Kevin Butler, a fourth-round draft pick out of Georgia. Butthead's addition had meant I had to let vet Bob Thomas go at the end of the preseason. Butler went on to set an NFL rookie scoring record in 1985, so Bob knew what he was up against. But I loved Bob Thomas. He was a great guy. Butler wasn't any more accurate, but he kicked off much deeper, so there was nothing I could do.

I didn't like cutting Bob. I never liked that part. I sat down with him, and it was miserable. It's the hardest thing you do as a coach. When I released defensive lineman Mike Hartenstine after 1986, it broke my heart. But there's a time when it has to happen, and you're the only one who can do it. Nobody teaches you how. I watched Coach Landry do it, and I watched him break down. I'd hear him tell a coach, "I'm keeping this man because he's a better football player, but I'm cutting a man who has so much more character." Oh, it hurt him!

I believe in loyalty. I thought about all that because we were playing without Bell and Harris, and people were saying the defense really missed them. It actually was tragic that they weren't with us, in a way. But you can't move on unless better players replace lesser ones, and the guys you have replace the guys you don't have. Loyalty only goes so far. Character only goes so far. Football is played with talent and speed and mean.

And I think Bob Thomas did okay, too, probably better than any of us. He went back to school, got his law degree, and now he's the chief justice of the Illinois Supreme Court.

Make no mistake about it—we were a talented team. Hell, we had 10 first-round draft picks on the club—a lot of them from Jim Finks and some from Jerry Vainisi and me. In the entire league, only the Packers had more first-round guys with 11.

One of our first-round guys, Mike Singletary, had a hell of a game, too. He had three sacks and an interception. What a competitor he was. What a student of the game. Another first-rounder, William Perry, our rookie 315-pound or 300-whatever-pound defensive tackle from Clemson, didn't get in much. But before the game the Patriots' center, Pete Brock, was asked about him. "That's an all-day sucker!" he said. But Buddy wasn't using Perry much. Big Bill already had his nickname, "The Refrigerator," and I felt we ought to plug that appliance in somewhere. Things were going through my mind. I was daydreaming and thinking and calculating.

Mostly, I was happy we got out of this one pretty easily. McMahon's back was a little stiff, so we rested him at the end and put in Fuller.

But there was no time to sit around and feel good about being 2–0. The NFL schedule was all about entertainment and not about sanity or what was good for us.

We had the badass Vikings in four days. ■

Chicago 27, Tampa Bay 19
Picked Up by a Pickoff

Once again the Bears struggled to get on track in a game they expected to win easily. In a near-replay of the season opener against Tampa Bay, the Bears trailed 12–3 at halftime and would have been shut out at intermission but for a 30-yard field goal by Kevin Butler as time expired in the second quarter.

It was not what the Bears had anticipated, certainly not against the winless Bucs. But there they were, looking up at the perennial doormats of the division. But just as they had in Game 1, the Bears used an interception to turn the momentum.

The first time it had been Leslie Frazier's pick. This time it was Dave Duerson breaking quickly on a ball intended for tight end Jimmy Giles, intercepting it and setting up a touchdown pass from

Jim McMahon to Dennis McKinnon covering 21 yards and pulling the Bears within 12–10.

The Bears then turned up the defensive pressure, and Tampa Bay quarterback Steve DeBerg pulled out from behind center too soon, leaving the ball on the ground. Defensive tackle Steve McMichael fell on it to set up another 30-yard Butler field goal to give the Bears their first lead.

They built the margin to 20–12 when Walter Payton, held under 100 yards rushing for the fourth straight game, scored on a four-yard run in the fourth quarter.

Tampa Bay answered with a 25-yard touchdown pass by DeBerg, his second of the game, and suddenly it was 20–19 with five minutes to go.

McMahon twice talked coach Mike Ditka out

Tampa Bay receiver Gerald Carter pays the price for a reception as Mike Singletary gets a closer look.

With two minutes left, McMahon anticipated a Bucs blitz and went deep to Willie Gault for 48 yards to the Tampa Bay 11. Payton scored two plays later to clinch the game with his second touchdown, this from nine yards.

The Bears were gaining confidence in their ability to rally using a variety of weapons, and Ditka was learning to let McMahon be McMahon. They were believing in their abilities, believing in their talent and, above all, believing in each other. ■

Chicago 27, Tampa Bay 19
OCT. 6, 1985, AT TAMPA STADIUM

BOTTOM LINE
Duerson's big play ignites turnaround

KEY PLAY
Emery Moorehead's 8-yard reception on third-and-3 with the Bears up by one late in the fourth quarter. It led to Walter Payton's victory-clinching touchdown run.

KEY STAT
Moorehead's eight receptions for 114 yards represented the best day by a Bears tight end since Mike Ditka.

of calling safe plays when it appeared that the easy way would be to punt and turn the game over to the defense. Instead McMahon converted a third-and-3 at the Bears' 24 with an 8-yard completion to Emery Moorehead to keep the ball and the drive alive.

Walter Payton and the Bears narrowly escaped with a win in the fifth game of their historic 1985 campaign (above). Jim McMahon eludes Bucs defensive end John Cannon on a day when the quarterback rushed for 46 yards (right).

DAN HAMPTON
No. 99, defensive end

"**O**ur Super Bowl was played against the Giants and then the Rams, because we knew once we got to the Super Bowl, it was an avalanche. No one was going to stop us."

"It was an amazing anticipation of all the expectations. Boom. It's done. It's over. We've done it."

"A lot of times people become overwhelmed and intimidated by something that explodes, and the next thing you know, it's on national TV. It was like Ditka took it in stride, saying, 'OK, that's great.' It's almost a Machiavellian way of using the Fridge on the *Monday Night Football* game. It's almost like he orchestrated it.

Buddy fostered an us-against-the-world mentality."

"The moment of truth was the Miami game, and you know about them grabbing each other in the shower and starting fisticuffs."

"Actually, Ditka was right. Ditka was right in saying, 'Hey, whatever you thought, it ain't working. You've got to change.'"

"When I played, everybody talked about the 'Steel Curtain' and the 'Doomsday Defense.' Now, 25 years later, they talk about the Bears' defense."

"You're not going to run it on us. When you try to throw it on us, it's just a matter of time before we start tearing your quarterback down."

"You have to give a lot of credit to Jim Finks in that he was able to build a roster of talent that Ditka was able to utilize."

"I had five operations on each leg when I played, and when I finished, I had both of them done again, so that's 12. I'll need some type of artificial joint when I'm 55 or 60. I couldn't run out of the house if it was on fire, but at the end of the day, I'm glad I was able to do what I was supposed to do."

"When I was in sixth grade, I'd fallen out of a tree and fractured both of my legs. I had played football, and I was obviously pretty gifted at it. But after I fell, they had to put pins and plates in my ankles. The doctor said I needed to do something else. I started playing saxophone in the band."

"I was very goal-driven, and the goal, obviously, is to go to the Super Bowl and win it. We

had it within our grasp, but we didn't close the deal, especially in '86 and '87."

"It's too simple to say, 'Oh, well, our quarterback was never healthy,' but I find it hard to believe that New England would've won three of four without Tom Brady."

"My problem with Jim McMahon was everybody had their own individual goals or objectives. I can't blame him for not having the same goals or objectives that I did. Every game was important, and every season is the most important. Jim had other ideas about how to go about it. He was looking at the long road, wanting a 15-year career."

"A lot of it came from the mentality of our team. McMichael and I and Ditka, we were Cro-Magnon. I think in a way that's what made that team special. The future doesn't belong to anybody. Today is the day."

"I've got a Hall of Fame ring and I've got a Super Bowl ring, and everybody says, 'Which do you like the most?' I said, 'Well, there's only [268] Hall of Fame rings in the world, but that's the only Chicago Bears Super Bowl ring there is.'" ■

chapter VI

A Dog on My Ankle

As we wrote this book, Ditka and I referred frequently to the loose-leaf 500-page binder that contained photocopied pages of Chicago newspaper sports reports from late 1984 all the way into early 1986. Sometimes Ditka would drift off, becoming so intent in his reading that his wife, Diana, and I would sit at the table in the restaurant, facing him, and talk about him almost as if he were not in the room. One time Mike borrowed his wife's reading glasses to see some particularly fine print, and Diana cracked up watching this huge, oblivious man with the big, ruddy, circular, mustachioed face, studying newsprint while wearing tiny, rhinestone-encrusted glasses.

Invariably Ditka would look up from his reading and say something about the craziness of that 1985 season, marveling at the whirlwind of gossip and excitement and anticipation and drama that surrounded the team and himself and how he was basically unaware of that sideshow element to the quest.

"I almost never read the papers," he said. "I never realized what was going on unless somebody told me. I guess we were a little different, huh?"

He did have a weekly TV show on CBS during the season—hosted by former Bears teammate Johnny Morris—that became something of a local legend, with fans going crazy during the tapings and nobody ever quite sure how any episode would end.

"McMahon doesn't practice. Now he's saying he thinks he hurt his back sleeping on his waterbed a week earlier. His waterbed. And he says he doesn't need to practice at all, all he needs is to know the game plan and different formations." —Ditka on McMahon

At 2–0 the frenzy knob was slowly being turned up for Ditka's boys, especially because there would be a third game in the first 17 days of the season—on a non-Thanksgiving Thursday, for goodness' sake—and the Bears were playing their third undefeated team in a row. (Yes, technically, Tampa Bay was unbeaten in the season opener.) Moreover, the Minnesota Vikings were a perennial spear in the side of the Bears, much like the Packers were. The Vikings had dignified history on their side with their icily stoic icon of a coach, Bud Grant, at the helm once again, after a year off. And the Vikes had been to four Super Bowls in the 19 years since the "ultimate game" began. The Bears, of course, had been to none.

Playing on a Thursday night, with one day being needed mostly for travel, was a tough chore for the Bears. But it was nothing compared to the distracting excitement after the Patriots game. For Ditka this was becoming a short week from hell. And the national media was starting to pay full attention to every tiny thing that came from the Bears camp, every word, every gesture, every bit of nonsense.

I didn't get crazy excited after the New England win, but I guess I shouldn't even have smiled. I thought McMahon had made it through in good shape. But there he was on Monday at Lake Forest Hospital, in traction.

I couldn't believe it.

I don't know when he hurt his back. And he didn't know for sure, either. It could have been from as far back as the Tuesday before the game. It could have been on the first play of the game. It could have been while opening beer cans. But there he was, again, hurt. The year before he missed seven regular-season games, plus the playoffs because of injuries. This uncertainty, I knew by now, would probably be a theme for Jim's whole career. It would probably make me check into a mental facility.

By Tuesday he was wearing a big immobilizing collar around his neck, but he couldn't practice, and I knew I was going to have to use Fuller, with Mike Tomczak as the backup quarterback. I mean, if you don't practice, how in the hell can you play? But right away Jim started yapping about how there was "no possibility" he wouldn't play. There were camera crews around. Joe Namath, Jim's old childhood hero, I guess, had come to town to do something for TV about Mac. This was a big national game we were playing, and I knew everybody was fired up. But I'd let McMahon play four games in 1984 with a broken hand, and we'd lost two and been trailing when he came out of another. If he was hurt now, he was out. This was my new rule. Jesus, the guy was too sore even for his chiropractor to work on him!

Other guys were banged up a little, too. Walter had bad ribs, maybe they were busted. But he never said anything, so I knew he was playing. Hell, he only missed one game in his entire career. And that was before I was coach, and he cried because they wouldn't let him in. He would never ask out of a game. You would have to cut his leg off for that to happen. Kurt Becker, one of our offensive linemen, was bruised pretty bad. Covert had no feeling in his right arm. Maybe a pinched nerve, who knew? Dennis McKinnon had a hip pointer, and he was still recovering from that off-season knee surgery. But he was a tough son of a bitch, too. He never said anything about pain, but I knew what a hip pointer was. I had one in college, and I played with it, and the muscle slipped off the edge and down into my abdomen. You keep playing with it, and you get injections, and when the painkillers wear off, it hurts so much you can't cough, you can't fart, you can barely sit.

The weird thing Dennis did, though, was he started talking about the Vikings. "I don't think they're as good as their record says," he said. Bulletin-board crap. Now I don't advocate stuff like that. But if you can back it up, I guess it's okay. And I wouldn't change anything about Dennis. I loved him.

We go up to Minneapolis on Wednesday because of the league's rule about being at the opposing site 24 hours in advance. This is a place I don't like, especially just three days after our last game. Guys are definitely sore and hurting. McMahon doesn't practice. Now he's saying he thinks he hurt his back sleeping on his waterbed a week earlier. His waterbed. And he says he doesn't need to practice at all, all he needs is to know the game plan and different formations. The media keeps asking me if McMahon is going to start. And I'm getting pissed off, and now I realize I actually want Fuller in there. He beat the Vikings the year before 34–3 when we clinched the division. He threw for two touchdowns. I'd like to show that he, Steve Fuller—and we—can do it again without McMahon at quarterback. So everybody shut up and sit down. Steve Fuller is my guy.

The game started, and the noise in that damn roller rink was out of control. I hate the Metrodome. But the hell with it. There was a bigger problem. We were getting our asses handed to us.

The offense was sputtering along, doing nothing. I could see that Walter was not himself. And all of the time we were falling behind, McMahon was bugging the shit out of me. He was pouting down on the bench, then he was standing behind me, then he was following me around like a puppy. I turned around and almost stepped on top of him. "Put me in," he was saying. "I can play. I'm fine."

He was driving me crazy! We hadn't practiced on Monday, then on Tuesday we were in shorts, no pads. We hadn't changed much in our game plan, because there was no time. This is what we do, and the coaches can't get pregnant with ideas. And Jim knew this. Get away from me! I'm thinking. But he's right there like a mosquito, just pestering me to death.

At halftime we're down 10–6. Then in the third quarter we close it to 10–9 on another Butler field goal, but Vikings quarterback Tommy Kramer throws a TD pass, and they're up, 17–9. All we've gotten after seven drives into their territory are three Butthead field goals. It isn't Fuller's fault, but things just aren't clicking.

"I can do it," McMahon is saying. He's driving me absolutely nuts.

"You can't throw the ball!" I say to him. "And you know you can't."

"You gotta put me in," he keeps saying. "I can throw."

"How can I put you in? You haven't practiced."

But he did go through warmups. I don't know how. But he did. That much was true.

"Put me in."

"I don't want you getting hurt all over again."

I wanted to win with Fuller. I thought about how we'd had to do it without McMahon before, and we'd probably have to again. I wanted to show we could do it for me, too. To prove to myself I didn't need him, that as a team, we really didn't need anybody.

Jim keeps standing beside me, then in front of me. Yapping away. The game's going on, and I'm trying to coach.

"Shut up!" I say. "We're trying to win!"

Then the third quarter's half over, and our ass is up against the wall. He's like a little rat terrier, this McMahon guy, biting my ankle.

"Okay," I say. "You're in."

I call a play, and I don't remember what it was, but McMahon gets to the line and I can tell

"Get away from me! I'm thinking. But he's right there like a mosquito, just pestering me to death." —Ditka on McMahon

he's calling an audible. Jesus. Lord help me, he's calling out "Blue-69," which is a weak-side takeoff for Willie Gault, a fly route.

Now the thing about McMahon is he has the uncanny ability to recognize a blitz just by reading the defense. He could look at a safety and know what was coming just from the safety's alignment, just from his eyes, just from his attitude and body language. So Willie takes off on the left side, and here comes the blitz. There was no way we could pick it up with our blocking. So Payton nails one guy really good and then takes just a piece out of the other guy. It was like bumper pool. McMahon's falling back, and at the last second he heaves the ball and, my God, it's a perfect pass, and Willie catches it for a 70-yard touchdown.

One play. Insane. The Vikings knew he couldn't throw. That's what I thought, too. But he did.

Then we get the ball back, and McMahon goes in and on the first play throws a 25-yard touchdown pass to McKinnon. Two plays, 95 yards passing, two touchdowns. I can't believe it. I have no idea how he's doing it. They are blitzing the crap out of him because they didn't think he could throw. They knew he couldn't throw, and they

knew his two touchdowns had to be luck. And then he throws another touchdown! This one a 43-yarder to McKinnon.

These are the busted-up Bears, remember? Are we tough? What do you think? McKinnon is just one of the guys who is playing hurt. I'll tell you something about him. There was a game in 1987 when we were playing the Giants at Soldier Field and I was sick of Lawrence Taylor coming off the line like he was running a 40-yard dash with track spikes on and a hot babe at the finish line. I called McKinnon aside and told him he was going to come in motion from the outside toward the tight end, and he was going to be set up on Taylor for a strong-side block. "And you're going to knock the shit out of him!" I added. L.T. went about 250 pounds and might have been the best defensive end or whatever he was, ever. Dennis went maybe 185, and his legs were beat and his arms were frail. You know what McKinnon said? "Okay." That simple.

He came in on a jog, then squared up and just sold out and hit Taylor as hard as he could and sent him flying. L.T. got up and looked at me on the sideline and yelled, "Ditka, you're an asshole!"

"What? I'm gonna let you run around and

"I truly wasn't concerned about the contract or security at that time. All I wanted to do was make the Old Man proud. Make myself proud."

—Ditka on 1984 contract negotiations

make every tackle?" I yelled back. "Watch out now. This guy's got balls and he's coming after you!"

Taylor's head was on a swivel the whole afternoon, and we negated his effectiveness. Dennis did, that is.

So anyway, back in the Minnesota game it's still the third quarter, five minutes have gone by, and this crazy McMahon has thrown for three touchdowns and we're ahead 30–17.

We won the game 33–24, Jim was the star of the hour, and I couldn't have been happier with that scrawny McKinnon, either. Payton said, "It was like everybody came in at halftime and got out their rosary beads."

I couldn't have prayed for anything like that. But what I was thinking was that if it hadn't been for our offensive line, none of this would have happened. If Walter hadn't hit those two blitzers, it wouldn't have happened. But here we are, and it did happen. I know we wouldn't have won that game without McMahon. We wouldn't have won the Super Bowl without him.

I had wanted to prove some stuff to myself,

but I had to back off and admit I was wrong. Joe Namath and all those ABC guys were there, and now the Bears were a big deal. Like I said, I didn't read the papers, but sometimes people told me what was going on. It was nothing new for me. The good guys were still good guys, and the assholes were still assholes. I mean, *Tribune* columnist Bernie Lincicome was still a jerk, what can I tell you? Writers started bugging me just to see what kind of a response they'd get. Sometimes I didn't handle it very well, but there are times when there isn't a good answer at all. Do you still cheat on your wife? I mean, help me out here.

I went on Channel 2 one time, and what's her name, Diann Burns, asked me a question, and I just flat out told her, "That's not a good question." Especially after a game, I needed a little time to come down, to cool the burners. I was better on Mondays than Sundays. Better Wednesdays than Mondays.

I'm not defending my behavior. Could I have handled things better in my career, like when I jumped all over Avellini or Harbaugh or yelled at reporters? Sure. But I handled it the way I knew how, and that's why I can't go back and apologize to anybody. McMahon called me Sybil, I've heard. Well, screw it—I didn't care what anybody said about me. I've always maintained that if your job isn't important to you, then don't do it. And my Bears job meant everything to me. I cared about what people said about my team, not me. It bothered me when I heard writers were writing bad stuff about the guys. I always felt like I was defending the entire history of the franchise.

I hate losing. I just do. Some things I can't win at. You want to challenge me in ballet or nuclear physics, you're going to win. But not in football. Not my Bears. Because I can do something about that.

It was like the season before, 1984, during the week leading up to the NFC Championship Game against the 49ers. The front-office guys wanted to redo my contract and sign me for another three years or something. I said, "Not now. We're coming up against the biggest game the Bears have had in years." It wasn't so I could negotiate better later. It was that I wanted no distractions. Michael McCaskey, the president, didn't seem to have a clue about that. He said, "I really want to announce it to the team, let them know you're going to be the coach for a long time."

I said, "They don't give a shit about that. They just want to play football."

Why was that so hard to understand?

We got whipped anyway. But I truly wasn't concerned about the contract or security at that time. All I wanted to do was make the Old Man proud. Make myself proud. Not make New Man McCaskey proud.

Now there was less time to think about any of that outside stuff. We were 3–0, and looking solid. I liked the fact that our offense had now bailed out our great defense in two of the three games. That made me feel good. I guess part of it was my competition with Buddy, my desire to make him know that our side of the ball was as valuable as his.

I was also glad we had 10 days off before we played the Redskins at home. We could use the time to heal, and I knew some of the guys could use the time to party a little bit.

McMahon probably wanted to party, but by the next day he was back in his favorite spot, the Lake Forest Hospital. Now besides his bad back, he had an infected leg bruise. He was in traction, and he had this lower-leg thing that was getting treated with heat and antibiotics and elevation. The doc thought Jim might have gotten the infection from a hand cut during an exhibition game.

I was beginning to think that waking up each morning was a dangerous thing for this reckless guy. Whatever. The Bears were now on the map. And after his game in Minneapolis, Jim McMahon was near the center of it all. ■

chapter VII

Yolanda Is Waiting, Meester Deetka

Dexter Manley, the Washington Redskins' unpredictable and loud-mouthed defensive end, said early in the week that even though quarterback Jim McMahon was a threat on offense, Walter Payton's running was more of a trouble spot for the 'Skins. "We're gonna have to knock Walter Payton out of the game," Manley said sweetly. "We're gonna have to do that." Not bad logic, perhaps. But not genius, either. And definitely not good pregame hype.

The entire Bears team was studded with special athletes, special personalities. Payton was, indeed, the most special of them all. The wily running back out of little Jackson State was now in his 11th NFL year, and he desperately wanted a championship ring before his time ran out. He had been the leading scorer in NCAA history when he left college, but he knew he needed to make his mark on the big stage, the NFL, to leave a grand legacy. In 1984 he had played in his seventh Pro Bowl, but he had been on mostly mediocre teams thus far in his career with the Bears—and that was why getting so close to the Super Bowl the year before had pained him so much. Time waits for no one. And as a not-so-big (5-foot-11, 205 pounds) workhorse tailback who had already carried the ball over 3,000 times in his pro career— Walter's clock was ticking fast.

"McMahon had recovered fairly well from his injuries—I mean at least he was upright and not in a body cast—and he came into the game almost like a real, non-limping quarterback." —Ditka on the Redskins game

A bigger problem for the Redskins, however, was their own record. They were 1–2 and had been wiped out in their season opener against the Cowboys 44–14 with quarterback Joe Theismann throwing five interceptions. Just the previous week they had nearly blown a 16–0 lead over the Houston Oilers before squeaking out a 16–13 win.

The Bears had beaten the Redskins 23–19 in last year's first-round playoff, but it had not been easy. Indeed, the Redskins had taken an intentional safety in the fourth quarter of that game, just on the chance of getting the ball back in better field position for a final run at a victory. The gamble failed, but the intent was there. Ditka was not complacent or certain about this fourth game. He worried about a blabbermouth like Manley, but most of all he worried about a shrewd coach like Washington's Joe Gibbs.

Anytime you play a Joe Gibbs-coached team, you worry. You know there's a lot going on in that mind, and you know he's thinking about stopping you. Joe retired years later, after winning the Super Bowl a couple times. Then he went on to be a car owner in NASCAR, and then I guess he got bored, because he came back to the NFL in 2004. He quit as the Redskins coach and president in 2008, and now he's an advisor for their owner, Dan Snyder. Whatever, he's no dummy, Joe Gibbs.

A season or so later, I said Manley had the IQ of a grapefruit. That was a dumb thing to say, but I didn't need to hear him flapping his mouth all the time. Hell, he had his own problems with drugs and other stuff, anyway. A columnist in Chicago said Manley "had the biggest mouth in a city of politicians," so that was about all you needed to know. And I was going to stand up for my guys against everyone, take the heat for them. When you're a team, it's like you're actually all part of the same person. If I took the heat, so what?

The thing that happened in the Washington game was that it got away from the Redskins real fast. Sometimes that happens when nobody expects it. They had a guy, Jeff Hayes, who was their kicker and punter, and he pulled a thigh muscle kicking off after they first scored, and that just ruined them. Willie Gault took off after he caught the kickoff, made some fakes, turned on the jets, and ran right past Hayes for a 99-yard touchdown to put us up 10–7. It was the beginning of the second quarter, and by halftime we were up 31–10. Thirty-one points in a quarter is pretty big. Let people say what they wanted about our offense. You go get 31 points in 15 minutes.

Right away Washington had to punt, and I wondered who they'd put back there, and this is wonderful, because it's Theismann. I'm thinking, "Look at that! That punt's gonna go behind him!" When the ball was finished doing whatever it was doing in the air, then on the ground, it actually netted one yard. After that their backup quarterback, Jay Schroeder, punted. But it was over. We destroyed Washington 45–10, their worst defeat in 24 years.

If you look at the stats from that game, they're deceptive. We only had 16 first downs and just 250 net yards on offense. They had 19 first downs and 376 net yards. And you know what? They did stop Payton. He only carried the ball seven times and gained six yards. But we were at our best, because we were opportunistic.

McMahon had recovered fairly well from his injuries—I mean at least he was upright and not in a body cast—and he came into the game almost like a real, non-limping quarterback. So you want to stop Walter, huh? Fine. Jimmy Mac hands him the ball and the whole Redskins team goes after Wally, and—la ti da—there goes Mac up the other sideline. Nobody's on him, because why should you care about a beat-up quarterback like him? He just jogs away from everybody like he's looking back, watching the play.

But Payton stops suddenly and throws a perfect spiral back across the field to McMahon, who runs in untouched for a 13-yard TD. That made it 28–10. Who cares if it's the wide receiver who scores on a pass or the quarterback? People can say we were fortunate in that game, but we made our own fortune. Where was grapefruit Manley when Payton threw the ball?

The thing is, Walter was such a great football player that you could do things with him that you couldn't with other backs. I think he could throw a football 70 yards. Hell, you think that touchdown pass to McMahon was his first in the NFL? It was his eighth! And he could punt. He did that for us a couple times in games. He could kick off. In college he kicked five field goals and over 50 extra points. When we really got busted up in one season, I even had him play at quarterback.

So far this season his stats weren't great—even though he caught a 33-yard touchdown pass from

McMahon later in the Redskins game—but we were winning. And his potential was always there. He could be the greatest decoy ever made. Think how much that helps a team. So far he had only 50 carries for 227 yards, which computed to about a 900-yard season. And he'd already had eight 1,000-yard seasons. He only missed going over 1,000 in his rookie year and in 1982, when there was a strike. But he had that pride that you couldn't kill. Nobody worked harder than he did getting in shape. He was the best conditioned athlete on our team. He was like a rock. If he had any

people may have thought he was hotdogging, but he never was a showboat, a hot dog, nothing. Never. You gotta have a little dislike for the other team, but you have to have respect, too, and I think Walter had the perfect mix. He respected all those guys trying to crush him, but he wanted them to know that the forearm to their chest or stiff arm right in their mouth was to prove they weren't bringing him down.

I mean, how big a heart did this guy have? The year before in the Washington game I said, "It's gonna be rough, Walter. We're not blocking them

"When he was breaking away from tacklers, he'd lift his legs up like a drum major." —Ditka on Payton

fat on him, you couldn't have grabbed it with pliers. He'd run that hill of his down in Mississippi, and I think he had a hill here in the Chicago suburbs, and he'd leave guys who were trying to stay with him half-dead, puking their guts out at the bottom.

In games after every run, he'd push the ball forward a few inches. The ref would move it back, but maybe over the course of his career Walter gained 50 yards that way. He had that high step, too. When he was breaking away from tacklers, he'd lift his legs up like a drum major. He did that in college, too. It was like his trademark. Some

very well."

He said, "Coach, just keep giving it to me. We'll pound 'em."

"I don't want you hurt," I said.

"They can't hurt me," he said. "I'm watching them. They can't hurt me."

He ran like a madman in that game. When we lost the next week to the 49ers in the NFC game, Walter was devastated. He was limping pretty bad afterward. A reporter asked him if he was hurt. "Not on the outside," he said.

Walter and I talked at times. But we didn't talk a lot. I'll tell you the truth—there wasn't a

Gary Fencik Remembers '85

The D-Line Beats Up the O-Line

"There was a battle between the defense and offense, but really it was mostly the front four going against the offensive line. That's how practices are.

"The defensive backs and linebackers might have drills, but even if you're doing seven-on-seven passing or recognition drills, you're not right on top of anybody. All the DBs are backed off, the linebackers are ready to drop back. You're not just pounding someone.

"But the defensive line and the offensive line are always going at it. Our defense knew it was good, and we didn't like to be beaten by anybody. Things would heat up and then there would be individual battles, and then Dan and Richard and those guys, they'd just get *pissed off*. So now they're hitting and it's intense. But I always felt it made our offensive line better. It was both sides trying to get better on the same drill, a tough thing.

"But there also was a deeper element, underneath everything. Buddy wouldn't call the defense off sometimes, and that built up this rivalry of defense versus offense. Buddy had been re-hired as defensive coordinator by George Halas before Halas hired Ditka to be head coach. That's highly unusual, to do it that way. Normally a head coach would hand-pick his assistant coaches. I mean, this was the founder and owner of the team who had done it. And I think it probably always was an issue. Buddy certainly would have liked to have been head coach, so the tension couldn't be avoided.

"I give Mike a lot of credit for the way he handled it all. The defense loved Buddy, and eventually it benefited us all."

whole lot to coach there. He was a complete football player. He knew everything, and if he didn't know, he'd just ask Suhey. Matt lined up in front of him a lot, to block—that's how Walter grabbed his shorts and his jockstrap that one time—and anything Walter didn't understand about a play, Matt would tell him. They had a great relationship. It was one of those really important relationships built on trust and having proved yourself to the other guy. Football teams, good ones, are full of small trusts like that. When they all come together, that's when you have a great team.

Take that Washington game. Yeah, they had guys injured and they lost their punter. But we had three starters out, too. Including Covert at left tackle. That's a pretty important position. But Andy Frederick came in and did a great job.

Now don't get me wrong about Payton. He sure as hell wasn't all serious and quiet. Everybody knows that. I didn't mind guys having their own personalities. God knows I was no altar boy when I was a player, and I didn't want a bunch of clones. But there was only one Walter, no matter what. Off the field he was beloved by the fans. I never once saw him say no to somebody looking for an autograph, to kids, to old folks, to the real people, anyway, not those frauds looking to get autographs and sell them. And he was a practical joker. If there was an explosion, you knew it was Walter. If a firework went off anywhere, anytime, you knew it was him. All kinds of stuff. He busted my balls all the time, and sometimes it was really good.

I remember I'd be in my office late at night and I'd get these phone calls. There'd be this Latino woman on the other end, and she had a thick Mexican accent and a real high voice and she'd say, "Meester Deetka, I am Yolanda. I am mucho caliente and I want to meet you at the motel down the street. I'm waiting for you! Pleez come, señor!"

I got these calls all the time, and then about a month later I found out it was Walter. I saw him at practice and I said, "You little prick!" God, he thought it was funny.

Now so many years later, I still think about him and what a tragedy it was when he died. It was only 1999, and he was still young. He was always so strong and healthy; it was just mind-blowing to see him wasted away. He used to have a grip that

was unreal, bring you to your knees. But what that liver cancer did to him was terrible. I never dreamed he'd be the first one to go from that team—before even any coaches. My offensive coordinator Ed Hughes died in 2000, and that was sad. But Walter? Going first? I remember a team doctor once told me early on that Payton's blood enzymes were a little screwed up, but what did that mean? It was no big deal. How could it be?

It just hurts for me to remember him being ill, losing his body that way. I spoke at his funeral, but I hate funerals. I want to celebrate life. I want to celebrate Walter Payton's life. He left a great wife, Connie, and their two wonderful kids. Man, he was a fun guy, I'm telling you.

And in 1985, he was obviously the guy who made our offense work. When I first took over in 1982, Buddy's defense seemed to just want to beat up our offense all the time. I'll say that again and again, because it's true. There were defensive players who didn't even know the names of the guys on offense. Didn't want to know. What good was that going to do for Walter? For all of us? Finally, I told Buddy that the Bears were not on our schedule. I guess I said that a few times through the early years. And now we had become a single unit—or at least the defense respected us. And knew our fricking names. Especially Payton's.

And why not? We already had scored 136 points, more than anybody in the league. We

Gary Fencik Remembers '85

"Robert" Dent

"I don't think the 'Robert' Dent thing was that big a deal. Ditka, you gotta love him, he said all kinds of stuff to everybody. He used to rip into cornerback Mike Richardson, for instance, saying, 'Mike Richardson, that guy don't know anything about defense!' The coaches called Richardson, 'L.A.,' for Los Angeles, saying he'd disappear in games when we played on the West Coast, where he was from. He's in the 'Super Bowl Shuffle' rapping

"Ditka would rip everybody after games, that was just routine. But he'd look at Richardson and say something like, 'But you—Mike—you actually did have a bad game.' It was all about energy. The Robert Dent thing, I mean, there were so many other ways Ditka could have offended him if he'd really wanted to."

needed to keep our consistency and togetherness. It bothered the defense a lot that Bell and Harris were apparently not coming back. And now Richard Dent was making noise about being underpaid. He'd made the Pro Bowl in 1984, just his second season, and he was underpaid at $90,000 a year. But we didn't need him asking to get traded, saying stuff like, "Maybe I can play somewhere else," right during the thick of things. Next year, maybe. Nah, not even then—just get it done in the off-season. Later on I called him Robert Dent, kind of as a joke. I probably shouldn't have done it—but it was a joke, people! Anyway, it was just my way of saying let's all keep pulling together, and nobody's name is that important. He wanted more publicity, so I gave it to him. But a Super Bowl ring is what it's all about, isn't it? Hell yes, it is. Already people were saying our offensive success was because of Jim McMahon and had nothing to do with me. Fine, I'll put that aside. Let's just keep rolling.

Things were going on around us, but I was oblivious. I think people don't realize how coaches are, how narrow they make their world. Look, I knew that John McEnroe was playing good tennis. And I knew Michael Jordan was this young kid for the Bulls, and he was starting his second season and he was amazing, but that was it. I look back and see that the Cubs couldn't get lights for night games at Wrigley Field. The Illinois Supreme Court said forget it. Of course, this was 20 years before Bob Thomas would run the court. Who knows what he would have ruled?

But I knew nothing about any of it, and I didn't care. It's pretty funny to see what Cubs president Dallas Green said. He was mad and said nobody would help the Cubs until it was crisis time, "And it will be crisis time next year when we have to play the playoffs and World Series in St.

Louis." Well, they didn't have to worry about that, did they? No, the Cubs are pretty consistent about not going all the way.

We had Tampa Bay to get ready for again. There wasn't a whole lot of news, except that everything we did seemed to get magnified in Chicago. William Perry weighed in at his semi-weekly weigh-in, and he was a sleek 314 pounds. That was down from 330 in training camp, and hip-hip-hooray! He made 1,000 bucks, or some-

that much on defense, and some media people—following Buddy's lead—were saying Fridge was a wasted draft pick. I sure didn't think so. He was fat. But underneath all that stuff was a hell of an athlete. I had seen how fast he was off the ball for a few yards, and I knew he could dunk a basketball. So we put ol' Fridge on the kickoff coverage team, and darned if he didn't make two tackles. Tampa Bay blockers weren't exactly thrilled to see this giant appliance rumbling their way.

"Things were going on around us, but I was oblivious. I think people don't realize how coaches are, how narrow they make their world." — Ditka

thing like that, every time he was under 315. The Fridge was unloaded! I remember later when he was getting really heavy, and he would tell me how he wasn't eating anything at all during the day. And he wasn't. But at night he might eat enough for five people. But he was a slender fellow in 1985, folks. He was a swizzle stick.

The Bucs game was a lousy one. We went down there and fell behind by 12 points and looked like crap. But Payton ran for two touchdowns, and we pulled it out 27–19. A win is a lot better than a loss, but Tampa Bay was 0–5, so how good could we feel? Buddy wasn't using Perry all

The bigger issue was that we'd been forced to come from behind in several of our games, and maybe that wasn't a good sign. But maybe, too, it meant we could beat people even when we weren't playing our best.

We'd find out soon. We were undefeated. But we traveled to San Francisco in six days, to play the world-champion San Francisco 49ers. We remembered them quite well. ■

Chicago 26, San Francisco 10
Payback Payoff: Memory Erased

It was time for some payback against the last team that had beaten the Bears, and this time the Bears were ready, unlike the last time they'd visited the Bay Area.

The Bears had been shut out and humiliated 23–0 by the 49ers in the 1984 NFC Championship Game, which left the Bears aware of how much higher they needed to go to gain elite status but also aware that it was within their reach.

The Bears simply crushed the 49ers, even if the score was still 19–10 with just under four minutes to play. They sacked Joe Montana seven times, the most of his career to that point, and San Francisco managed only 45 total yards and three first downs in the second half.

But the story for the Bears was on offense, where Walter Payton and the line clicked into a new gear. Payton rushed for 132 yards, his season high so far, and carried the ball 24 times in the kind of performance that had been missing.

Significantly, the Bears opened the game passing, despite being without Dennis McKinnon and Emery Moorehead because of injuries. Jim McMahon accounted for 115 passing yards in the first quarter, and the offense scored the first four times it had the ball. Payton scored on a three-yard run, and Kevin Butler converted three straight field goals as the Bears breezed to a 16–0 lead.

But the 49ers were Super Bowl champs, and Carlton Williamson returned an interception 43 yards for San Francisco's first score before Ray Wersching kicked a field goal from 32 yards.

Willie Gault tries to control one of his three catches against the 49ers.

had inserted guard Guy McIntyre as a fullback in the closing minutes of the title game. Ditka sent in defensive tackle William Perry as a running back and had him carry the ball on the final two plays, picking up two yards on each rush. The game ended, but Perry's time in the spotlight was only beginning. ∎

Chicago 26, San Francisco 10
OCT. 13, 1985, AT CANDLESTICK PARK

BOTTOM LINE
Payton, Butler star; Montana takes a licking

KEY PLAY In an affront to 49ers coach Bill Walsh, William Perry debuted at fullback on the final two plays of the game.

KEY STAT Bears held offensive guru Walsh's attack without a touchdown for just the second time in his career.

But that was all the 49ers could manage against a team determined to get some payback for the 1984 thrashing. The Bears put away the game on a 29-yard Butler field goal in the fourth quarter and Payton's 17-yard touchdown run.

Coach Mike Ditka got a bit of payback of his own against San Francisco coach Bill Walsh, who

San Francisco coach Bill Walsh congratulates Mike Ditka after the Bears' victory (above). Bears running back Walter Payton breaks through a line of players for an 11-yard gain as San Francisco 49ers defensive end Jeff Stover (72) tries to bring Payton down on October 13, 1985, in San Francisco (right).

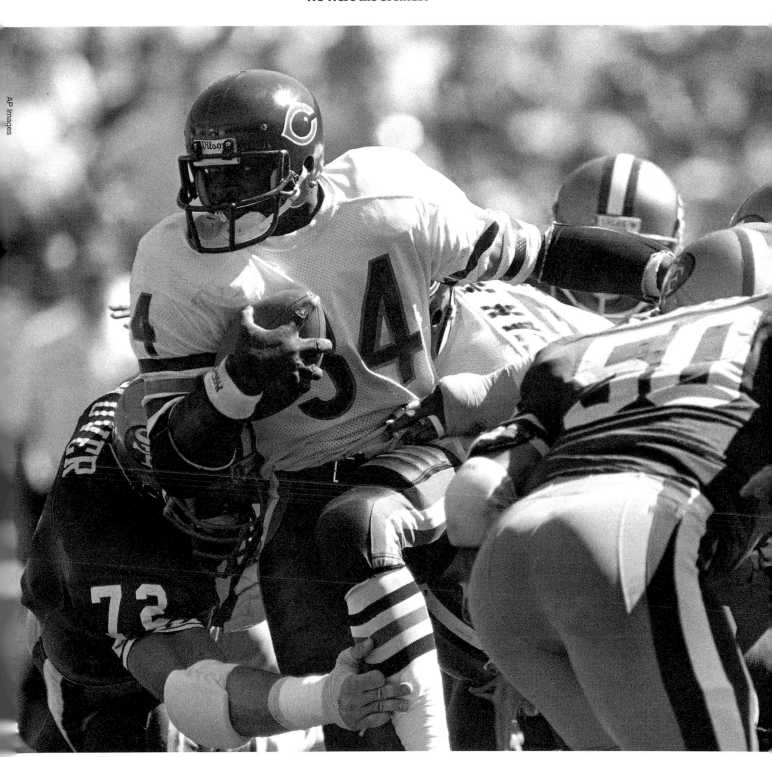

AP Images

WILLIAM PERRY

No. 72, defensive tackle

"It's still the same. People see me and say hello, say, 'That's the Fridge.' Take a picture."

———————

"It started in San Francisco. That's when I first ran the ball. Then on *Monday Night Football* [against the Packers] that's where it all blew up and everybody saw me and took to me, and everything happened after that."

———————

"I was a running back way back in the day, but you get to professional ball and you can score touchdowns and all, now it's just funny to me."

———————

"That was one crazy play [when he was in the backfield against Dallas]. I was supposed to go out and block on the cornerback. I went out and blocked on Everson Walls. Walter was going up the middle. I went and blocked on Walls, and we was out there talkin' for a few seconds, and I look back and everybody was on Walter. I went back into the crowd that was tackling Walter and knocked everybody off and grabbed him and pulled him into the end zone. The referee said, 'You can't do that! You can't do that!' I said, 'It's done now.'"

"I couldn't say too much about Walter. He was a great guy, a class act, a wonderful person on and off the field. We spent plenty of time going out to his places, his clubs, played pickup basketball together."

———————

"To me, Mike Ditka was a wonderful guy, a wonderful coach, a nice person, a great all-around guy. He's the one that drafted me, and I appreciated that. He's the one that gave me a chance and put me in the backfield and stuff. I still love him and appreciate him and give him the utmost respect."

———————

"My mother told me not to talk about people unless I can say something good about them. My mom and my dad brought 12 of us up, eight brothers and four sisters. She taught us well. She passed about 20 years ago. Most of us are having a great life. Some passed, and they had a great life. That's why I say enjoy yourself; you never know what goes on."

———————

"Money is nothing. You can't take it with you when you go to heaven. I use it as a tool to keep going."

"I let them talk about [my weight]. I was happy then. I'm happy now."

———————

"The nickname came from Clemson. Me and the guys, we went out one night, having a couple beers, and we came back and there was an elevator in our dormitory. I was so big then and I walked through it, and a light was hanging down, and the guy behind me said, 'You ain't nothing but a walking refrigerator,' and that's how I got the name."

"You've got to say the favorite moment was scoring a touchdown in the Super Bowl. That's what you work for the whole time, from peewee ball all the way through. You get the chance to score a touchdown, so I can't say no more. That was the highlight of the whole thing." ■

chapter VIII

Sic 'Em Fridge, and the Premature Celebration

All week long 49ers coach Bill Walsh praised the Bears, saying their offense was "exceptionally well-designed," and basically magnificent and untouchable, and their defense "was possibly the most effective defense in football." Ditka was even more congratulatory and effusive, difficult as that might seem. The Bears coach came close to fainting, his bodice was so tight. San Francisco had "the most intimidating defense I've ever seen," he said. And it had "the most innovative offense that's ever been." Ditka didn't say he thought Bill Walsh was God, but it might have been on his mind. Ditka hoped against hope that his Bears wouldn't get "blown out of the city." Gentlemen, grab your barf bags.

Ever the man with an intuitive grasp of the absurd, Ditka told newsmen he had even considered calling NFL commissioner Pete Rozelle. "What if we both didn't show up?" he asked.

San Francisco, though 3–2, still had the highest rating in the silly Dunkel NFL Index, but the Bears were No. 3, right behind the runner-up Miami Dolphins. "Did they announce it yet?" Ditka said at his Thursday press conference. "The game's been canceled. Mutual fear."

"I told him to go in and tell McMahon he was running the ball. Just grab the ball, hold it like a sack of money, and head south." —Ditka on Fridge's first carry

But the rematch of the NFC Championship Game contenders was on. Same field. Same coaches. But one team had a different quarterback. Jim McMahon. And Ditka himself was certain he had learned from the embarrassing defeat the season before.

Fans at that January NFC title game out in San Francisco had been screaming at us, "When you come back, bring an offense!" It was a fair thing to yell. I had thought we could play conservatively, hang around, and win with our defense in that game. I found out we couldn't. So we came ready to roll this time. We wanted the other team to be intimidated. We wanted to establish some fear if we could. Lots of it.

This was our offense, doing things right. Walter came out and he was pumped up, to say the least. He rushed for 132 yards and he scored two touchdowns. The last one, in the fourth quarter, he carried two 49ers around the left end with him right into the end zone. It was a 17-yard sweep and it put us up 26–10, and that was the final score.

We played without Dennis McKinnon and tight end Emery Moorehead, because they were injured, and used backups Ken Margerum and Tim Wrightman to fill in. They did fine. Hell, we scored the first four times we had the ball. Our offensive line was exploding off the ball and blocking like crazy. And, of course, our great defense was there. I don't think Walsh and his guys knew what hit them. Joe Montana was sacked seven times, the most in his career, and they only got 183 net yards, not even half their average.

Like I said, we had a big chip on our shoulder from the year before. Payton told the press afterward that the 49ers hadn't shown us much "courtesy or dignity" when they beat us before and also that they said "negative things about our offense." That made me smile a little. But we already had gotten the last laugh.

We had that 26–10 lead, and our defense had stopped them again, naturally, and we were running out the clock to end the game. Well, let's pause for a moment.

I remembered when Walsh put that big load McIntyre in the backfield the year before, and how I didn't much appreciate it. Plus, I like to be a little—what do you want to call it?—creative? So I called Fridge over, and we had a little conference.

"The problem was Buddy saw this as a slap in the face. That wasn't how I meant it. It just made us a better football team." —Ditka on Fridge playing offense

He was at attention and was like, "Okay, Coach! Yessir, Coach!" I told him to go in and tell McMahon he was running the ball. Just grab the ball, hold it like a sack of money, and head south. We hadn't practiced Fridge running or put anything in the playbook about it. But the guys might have had an idea I was going to try something different. Perry went thundering off at full speed, screaming to the ref that he was reporting to the backfield and yelling to McMahon that he was now a running back. I didn't know what Buddy was thinking about this, but what the hell. If the defense isn't going to use this guy, I'm gonna. I knew Bill Walsh would appreciate it.

So McMahon gave Perry the ball, and Fridge crashed straight into the line. Our offensive linemen were terrified he might fall on them. Hilgenberg used a cut block on his man just to get down and out of the way. We gave the ball to Fridge on the next play, too, and it was just another huge collision. I don't think the defenders knew what the hell was happening. I know they weren't crazy about tackling Big Bill. Their safety Carlton Williamson said afterward he personally was "a little upset about it."

Hey, screw 'em! It's football. If you can kick somebody's ass, shouldn't you do it? It was revenge for me. Yeah, I'll admit it. A little bit. Maybe a lot. Even though my first thought about using Fridge back there was this big fellow can really block. I'd watch him in sprints in practice, and for the first five yards or so there was all this dirt flying up from under his shoes. Looked like a roto-tiller. I didn't like it when they used McIntyre in the backfield against us, that's for sure. So here's a response.

Buddy had his favorites, which is okay, because he was one of those old coaches who believes you have to earn your spurs and that rookies generally can't play. He really believed players had to earn the right to be out there. Being the first draft choice, like Perry, meant nothing to him. But Buddy was dead wrong about Perry and his abilities. Buddy didn't even want us to draft him. He called him "Fatso" or just "Number 72." Fine, I'll take the big kid. And I did.

The problem was Buddy saw this as a slap in the face. That wasn't how I meant it. It just made us a better football team, I thought. Okay, and it was fun. I guarantee you goal-line practices became a lot more fun with Fridge back there. And I started thinking of other things to do with him. Back then, remember, a huge player was like 275 pounds. Three-fourteen? Three-thirty? It was crazy.

So now we are all the rage. We are the sideshow. It had been building, and the Minnesota game got everybody's attention, and McMahon and Payton and Singletary were pretty well known. But this was big. In four days we're going to be on the cover of *Sports Illustrated*. Well, McMahon was on it, throwing a pass over a San Francisco

A lot of people thought it was nuts when I was hired to coach the team. But when Mr. Halas hired me, he didn't hire me for Xs and Os. He hired me because I was a Bear. His own family didn't have anybody like me in it. They weren't football people. The McCaskeys didn't play. I think Halas hired me because he had a gut instinct, and he followed it. When I first arrived, he asked me what I wanted to do for my staff, if I had people in mind.

"I have a few," I said.

"A lot of people thought it was nuts when I was hired to coach the team. But when Mr. Halas hired me, he didn't hire me for Xs and Os. He hired me because I was a Bear." —Ditka

player, above the headline, "BEARS ON THE PROWL: Jim McMahon Leads Undefeated Chicago Past the 49ers."

I felt pretty good. I felt I had redeemed our team from the embarrassment of the year before. Well, they had done it. I am certain we had more talent than anybody. But talent doesn't always win. The sideshow stuff didn't affect me, it wasn't important to me. I wanted to be proud of being a coach for this team and city I loved. You only get a few opportunities in life, that's it, and you better grab them.

Then he said, "I would really like you to keep the defensive coaches."

"Why?" I said.

"Because that's a very strong part of our football team. Buddy Ryan came here in 1978, and the players like him and they play hard for him."

"Fine," I said. "I have no problem at all with that." I meant it.

I only brought in a couple of coaches, mainly Ed Hughes, whom I'd been with for a few years in Dallas, to be offensive coordinator. Buddy was a hell of a coach. But I know he thought he should

have been named head coach. There was nothing I could do about that. You have to understand that when I first got there, the Bears defense was much, much better than the offense. We had to build the offense little by little, put the pieces of the puzzle in place. But it was hard to do when we were practicing against those guys and they were going full speed and we couldn't accomplish anything. They were better than us, cut and dried. Understand? So what? Buddy and I would have the argument constantly, over and over and over. We don't play the Bears, Buddy. I don't see them on our schedule. Do you? Where? We have to play the other team's defense, not ours! The attitude and respect changed after Covert body-slammed McMichael. And after Fridge played against San Francisco, too. But still I had to tell Buddy to put William in on defense. I mean, this guy was a good athlete. He didn't deserve the rap of being just a fat guy, and he sure as hell wasn't lazy.

I wanted Buddy to know we could not win if we had different goals. The only goal should be the whole team's success. But I saw him get caught up in stats and sacks and stuff like that. I mean, why were we blitzing when we're up 21 points? Because we're the No. 1-rated defense and we want more sacks. So I was going to use one of his defensive players when I wanted to.

And I felt good and celebrated just a bit after our win. We got on the plane, and I started drinking wine with Jerry Vainisi. I mean, it wasn't like we were crazy celebrating. I was just relishing the little bit we'd accomplished. It's a long flight from California, and the wine kept coming. We felt good and we were dissecting the game, enjoying the glow. When we got to O'Hare early in the morning, everybody went scrambling for their cars. I got in mine and took off and headed north on I-294.

All of a sudden I see a police light turn on, and the next thing I know, I pull over and the guy is giving me a ticket for driving under the influence. I was wrong, and driving after drinking is a terrible thing. But the guy was a prick. I was 100 percent wrong, I admit that. But here I am on the side of the highway, and players are flying past in their cars and they're looking at their coach getting arrested. I think a player or two stopped, and I told them to keep on going. I didn't think I was drunk. My judgment was good, but maybe it wasn't perfect. I argue with that cop, call him everything I can think of. Everything in the book. It's not a good scene.

I did everything I was supposed to do, though I didn't take a breathalyzer, because I didn't want to. Tom Landry called me during the week, and I appreciated that. We talked all the time, anyway, but he just called to give me support. He told the press I was a "good man," and that was nice.

I came in and gave a talk to the players on Monday, apologizing to them, to the organization, for my

Gary Fencik Remembers '85

William Perry and the Makeup of the '85 Team

"Fridge was a big story, so to speak—don't get me wrong. But most rookies don't make big contributions on veteran NFL teams. The bigger story, at least at the start, was Todd Bell and Al Harris not coming back. I mean that was huge. They had been so good in 1984. We're thinking: We can go to the Super Bowl without Todd, our All Pro strong safety, and without Al, our No. 1 pick and outside linebacker? How can we even make it to the Super Bowl, let alone win it?

"We all knew we had one shot to win, and we wanted all hands on deck. This was just really bad news. But you know what? Dave Duerson stepped in for Todd and made the Pro Bowl, and Wilber Marshall filled in for Al, and he did a terrific job and he made the Pro Bowl three times after that. Give Buddy and Mike credit. It really was we're gonna play with who we have and nobody will get in our way.

"But when I think of William Perry that year, the first thing I always think of is he was just such a good-natured guy. He could have been a jerk, a first-round pick and all, but he wasn't and the team really embraced him. All the hoopla, all the stuff about not being used that much at first on defense and then doing all that stuff on offense, it didn't seem to faze him. He was a genuinely nice, and, of course, very athletic guy. We played basketball sometimes, and did you ever see him jam? It was remarkable the spring he had.

"He just fit in with everybody so well. And then to see him carry the ball or whatever Ditka would have him do? When there was a goal line drive by our offense in a game, the defense usually wouldn't be watching. We'd be getting ready to go back in, getting prepared as a unit. I can guarantee you when Fridge was in the backfield, *everybody* was watching."

behavior. They needed to forgive me, and I didn't need my authority undercut. And we sure didn't need any more distractions on our road to the postseason. So I wanted to get this all behind me.

Some press guy told Darryl Rogers, the Detroit Lions head coach, what I'd done, and Darryl said, "I guess I'd probably do that, too."

Darryl doesn't drink. And the press guy reminded him he didn't drink, in case he'd forgotten.

"But I would if we were 6–0," said Darryl.

Yes, we were still undefeated. And it was Packer week. And nobody who calls himself a Chicago Bear can relax during Packer week. I know I didn't. ∎

Chicago 23, Green Bay 7
Refrigerator in the Living Room

What had begun as an in-your-face gesture from Mike Ditka to Bill Walsh in Game 6 reached international proportions eight days later when William Perry, in front of a *Monday Night Football* audience, obliterated a Green Bay linebacker while blocking on two Walter Payton touchdowns and scored one of his own.

The Bears again trailed initially as Green Bay scored on a 27-yard pass from Lynn Dickey to James Lofton. But in the second quarter, the Bears exploded on the Packers, scoring 21 of the more memorable points in an absolutely memorable year.

With a first-and-goal situation at the Green Bay 2-yard line, Perry ran onto the field and lined up behind right tackle Keith Van Horne, with Payton behind Jim McMahon in the backfield. Perry then led Payton into the hole and met Green Bay linebacker George Cumby, who was at a 100-pound disadvantage. Perry bent Cumby backward, and Payton scored easily.

Several minutes later the Bears drove to the Green Bay 1-yard line, and Ditka again sent in Perry. But this time Perry was not blocking for Payton. Instead McMahon handed the ball to Perry, who rumbled into the end zone and then spiked the ball.

He was not finished. The Bears pushed the Packers backward one more time in the second quarter and again stood at the Green Bay 1. Ditka motioned to Perry, and the big rookie lumbered onto the field for a third time. Perry lined up behind the left guard and tackle and again found

After William Perry's crushing block, Walter Payton flies over the goal line in the second quarter.

110

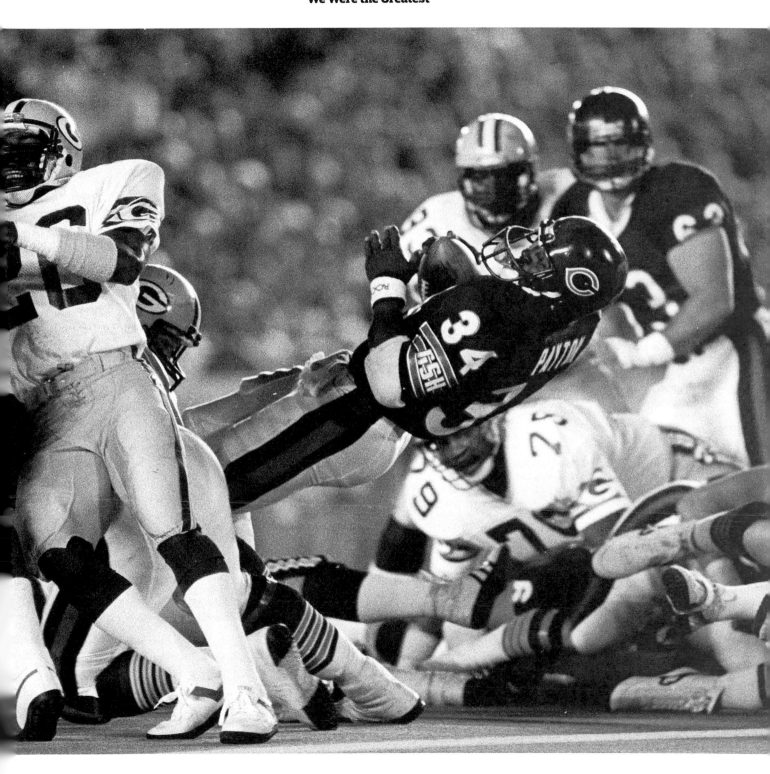

times, losing four, but still outgained Green Bay 342-319. They held the Packers to 96 rushing yards while pounding the Packers for 175 of their own. McMahon completed only 12 of 26 passes for 144 yards, but the Bears intercepted four Green Bay passes to take away any offensive consistency from their guests.

But the night had belonged to Perry. ■

Chicago 23, Green Bay 7
OCT. 21, 1985, AT SOLDIER FIELD

BOTTOM LINE
Perry phenomenon too much for Packers

KEY PLAY
William Perry's one-yard plunge in the second quarter, breaking a 7–7 tie. He also twice opened gargantuan holes for Walter Payton to score.

KEY STAT
The Bears intercepted Green Bay quarterbacks Lynn Dickey and Randy Wright four times and knocked both out of the game.

Cumby in the way, but not for long. Another crunching hit and Payton eased in for his second touchdown and one of his 112 rushing yards.

That was the end of the scoring by either offense, though Otis Wilson added the game's final points with a sack of backup quarterback Jim Zorn in the fourth quarter. The Bears fumbled seven

Randy Scott, who led the '85 Packers in tackles, separates Emery Moorehead from a second-quarter pass (above). William "Refrigerator" Perry (72) helps an unidentified teammate to his feet in the second quarter of the Monday night game in Chicago on October 21, 1985 (right).

EMERY MOOREHEAD

No. 87, tight end

"**O**ur team, everybody knew we were going to the Super Bowl. After we lost to the 49ers the year before in the NFC Championship, Mike Ditka made a point of saying, 'Remember this. We're going to be back.' [Dan] Hampton I remember saying, 'We're going to win the damn thing next year.' Everybody came back with a purpose."

———————

"I remember being in the locker room and everybody being ecstatic. But it was a situation where we knew we were going to win. We expected to win. We really did."

———————

"Ditka, I think, was a pretty good coach. He was a great motivator. Not a great tactician, but certainly a great motivator of men. He got the best out of everybody."

———————

"We led the league in rushing. We led the league in time of possession. We were underrated as an offense because the defense was just phenomenal."

———————

"Walter Payton was an iron man out there. He played with pain. Throwing up in the huddle. The guy loved to play football and loved to play every down."

"Our line, we always had a lot of good surges, trying to get out of the Fridge's way."

———————

"Bears fans, most of them still think you play. It's crazy. They think you're still 30 years old or whatever. The comment most often is 'You should be playing' and 'They haven't had a tight end since you left.'"

———————

"Having been born and raised in Evanston, I certainly could appreciate it a little bit more than some of the other players winning the Super Bowl and how long it had been since the city had won a championship. My father was a garbage man for Evanston. My mother worked at the post office for years. Just a typical family from Evanston. Blue-collar family that worked. Every kid wanted to be Dick Butkus and Gale Sayers."

———————

"Myself, always being a die-hard Cubs fan, Ernie Banks was No. 1 over everything. I was at a dinner, and Ernie was in the back telling stories and signing autographs. I waited until everybody had talked to him, and then I went up and introduced myself. It was like I was a little kid again. I was in my 30s." ∎

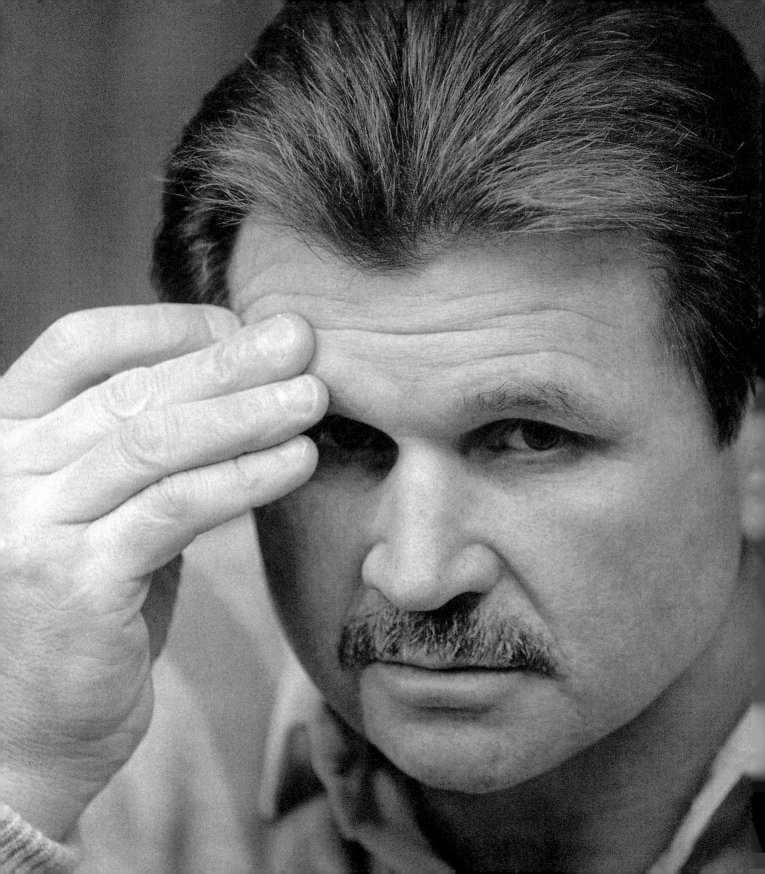

chapter IX

Hit Lists in Cheeseland, the Marvelous Mudslide, Halfway Home

The Green Bay Packers and Bears have played, as of this writing, 179 times. The two teams are separated by about 175 miles, many different heroes, villains, successes, failures, and—as Wisconsinites will quickly remind those from down south—the Illinois state line. That border, their T-shirts will tell you, is the difference between "a Cheesehead and a ——head." Being in the NFC Central and vying for the same title year after year since George Halas and Curly Lambeau were young men have made the battles between Green Bay and Chicago especially spirited. If that's the word. Hate *comes to mind. Or at least it did when Ditka's teams played.*

"I never really disliked anybody up there. Respect is important, more than hatred." —Ditka on Green Bay

The Bears of 1985 were already a major success. They were undefeated, of course. But now they were becoming more of an attraction, a media fascination, R-rated variety show, so to speak. They were something new in the sports field, entertainment in and of themselves, complete and self-contained. All they needed was the random foe. Ditka would never put it that way. He worried as he coached. But this first Packers game of the season was in Chicago, on the shores of Lake Michigan, at artificial-turf-clad Soldier Field, and that soothed him some. It was a homecoming of sorts, because the Bears had been on the road the last two games. And it was the team's first foray of the season into the fiery-hot glare of ABC's monumentally rated Monday Night Football. *The scene was set for something dramatic—or at least melodramatic—to happen. Ditka would never let folks down.*

Now, you have to understand I don't hate the Packers. The Old Man had tried to instill that in me, the hatred—he tried to drum it in to me. But I never hated the Packers. I never wanted to kill them or see them as mortal enemies. I respected those players, because I knew that they were part of a great organization, one of the best, as far as I'm concerned. At least under Lombardi they sure were. I never really disliked anybody up there. Respect is important, more than hatred. I never even disliked the Green Bay fans. They always treated me pretty well, even with all of the booing. They could get on me at Lambeau Field pretty damn good, but this game was at Soldier Field, our home.

If there was an issue at all, it was that we wanted to go all the way this year, and Green Bay was a roadblock in our path. Also, their coach was Forrest Gregg, a guy I'd played against when he was with the Packers and I was with the Bears, and I knew him pretty well.

I liked Forrest Gregg. I mean I never disliked him. Didn't hate him. But the year before, in the preseason, we were playing them up in Milwaukee at the Shriner's Game thing, and they were going to win the game—I mean, it's just August and we're looking at different players—and he did some stuff at the end of the game I didn't appreciate. The game was over, for all intents and purposes, and they were trying to score or something—why I don't know—and I told the press afterward that it was stupid, that he was stupid, that all that could happen was somebody would get hurt doing this stupid crap.

I know I was wrong to say anything. It was football. But he got pissed off at me, and then I got pissed off at him, and it lingered through all of 1984. But this game was important. Just to win, the hell with Forrest Gregg. Here was the thing. During the week I actually put in plays for William Perry at fullback, plays we practiced. I had already used him as a runner to kill the clock, and the world went nuts. Let's see how the world liked having him block, too. And, hmm, what about this mammoth guy, the guy Hampton had nicknamed "Biscuit"—because he was a biscuit over 350 in training camp—actually scoring? Fridge, the touchdown-maker. I liked the concept.

We started out like crap, fumbling three times, and the Packers took the lead 7–0. It was the second quarter and we finally started to move, getting down to the Green Bay 2-yard line. I yelled, "William, get in there!" Out Perry rumbles, and the Monday Night crowd goes bananas. He lined up over right tackle and made the lead block for Walter. He hit Packers linebacker George Cumby and he just, I don't know, absorbed the poor guy. Cumby weighed 90 pounds less than Fridge, and he took him on high and, my God, I thought they'd end up in Michigan. Walter scored like it was nothing, like he was eating an apple at a picnic.

Not long after that we got down to the goal line again, and I signaled for Fridge to get out there. He went out and lined up behind right tackle, as usual. But this time Jim handed him the ball. Fridge charged into the blockers and dove across the goal line like I guess he'd seen Walter do before. I thought the end zone would tilt. I mean this guy has a 22-inch neck, wears a size 58 coat. He could bench 465. Ray Sons wrote after the game in the *Sun-Times* that it was "the best use of fat since the invention of bacon."

Now the crowd is truly nuts. I can tell the difference in the sound. Perry has turned the game around, and football fans everywhere are watching and enjoying this. Call it a sideshow. I called it beating their ass. Think about it. How would you stop a man that size coming directly at you?

With a little more than a minute left in the half, we get down to the goal line one more time. I fiddle around and send in a couple of other substitutes. Everybody is chanting, "Per-ree! Per-ree!" I know what they want, but let's tease this for just a second. What the hell, it's entertainment, isn't it? Okay, Fridge, get on out there! Now McMahon is waving his arms in circles, getting the roaring crowd even more pumped up. Perry lines up on the other side this time, just for the variation, over left tackle, and I can see poor Cumby is across from him once again. He has to follow because of their defensive scheme or whatever. Mac gives the ball to Payton, who follows behind Fridge, who obliterates Cumby once more.

"I felt like I was stealing," is what Walter said afterward about the touchdown. Cumby said something about how he thought about taking on one side of Perry, but it didn't matter because "one side is as big as another."

We were ahead 21–7, and a legend was being built. We went on to win 23–7 after Otis Wilson sacked their third quarterback, Jim Zorn, for a

well. . . . But in life, we learn and we move on.

Things changed. William Perry was booked to be on David Letterman, and he was getting offers to do ads, T-shirts, posters, endorsements, all kinds of things. I heard somebody was even talking about a toy robot of Fridgie. Maybe they could have called it by the other nickname Hampton gave him, "Mudslide." And pretty soon Buddy started using

"Who would have guessed that in 25 years there would be 300-pounders everywhere in the NFL and people even bigger than Fridge just walking down the streets?" —Ditka

safety at the end. Naturally, we had beaten up all of their quarterbacks. Just abused them. Five sacks. That's just the way the D was.

It was a good show, and I think it helped get everybody's mind off of the humbling week the head coach had had. Yeah, it had been a humiliating thing, and maybe it just showed I could make mistakes like anybody. Was I perfect? No. But we're flying back from a huge win, we're at 35,000 feet for four hours, there's some wine, we have that good feeling you get from doing something

him on defense, moving Hampton to end and sitting Mike Hartenstine more. I won't say Buddy was surrendering. He would never use that word, never say it. But he backed off a little because he realized Perry deserved to be on the field and that his defensive line needed relief at times.

In fact, with a guy like Perry, the NFL was actually changing, moving to a new place. There were only a couple big guys back when I played, guys like Les Bingaman. But I hardly remember anybody being over 300 or even close to 300. In

Gary Fencik Remembers '85

Fridge Levels George Cumby

"I think the safety went down on one of those plays, just to get out of the way of Fridge. What could you do? And the linebackers are there, and I think Cumby went back so far he hit the goal post.

"Using William that way was absolutely a response to Bill Walsh using Guy McIntyre in the backfield for the 49ers. It was very smart. The offense practiced that play before the Green Bay game and then of course there were variations later on. Fridge would go over from defense to the goal line offense and we'd be wondering what this guy was doing over there and why Ditka had him lined up with Walter in the backfield. I wondered if we were really going to use that play. They did.

"Poor Cumby."

1985 America liked this fat stuff. It appealed to the regular guy. It was a novelty. Who would have guessed that in 25 years there would be 300-pounders everywhere in the NFL and people even bigger than Fridge just walking down the streets?

My main concern was still injuries—injuries to Jim McMahon more than anybody else. Keeping him healthy was almost impossible. He practiced like a lineman. He showed little or no regard for his body. I really think he was trying to prove to his teammates that, "Hey, I am the toughest guy out here." I think a lot of offensive players bought into what he was doing. Jesus, he'd do head butts with Van Horne, bad neck, bad back and all! Even the defensive players bought into it. This guy was crazy, in a football way, and they couldn't help but appreciate that.

Whether you liked Jim McMahon or not, he was a tough football player and a good leader by example. He was kind of nuts, but I think ultimately he was respected by everybody on our team. He drove me insane and he pissed me off. I guarantee you he and Hampton didn't get along. But he could lead, because deep down inside all that stuff, he had a brilliant football mind. He had a near photographic memory for downs, situations, blitzes, alignments, weaknesses, all of it. But I think he is wacky, and I think he didn't cultivate it. His different drum beat was he had an authority problem—me, his dad, his head football coach in college, Lavelle Edwards. He was a Catholic and he went to BYU—all Mormons—and I heard BYU never forgot, either. I'll bet he tested that program

more than anyone in history. He had his own problems, and he has worked on those throughout his life. And as I said, we all make mistakes. But he was what he was. And we rode it. When we could.

Coming into the week of the second Minnesota game, Jim had a bruised arm, a sprained ankle, and a sore butt cheek that was black and blue and hemorrhaging. Would he be able to play? Who knew?

As it turned out, he did play, and the O-line kept him off his posterior. Wally ran for over 100 yards, and Fridge played for the first time at nose tackle, on first downs, precisely why we drafted him. He got his first sack, too, when he nailed Tommy Kramer on their opening possession. I didn't even use him on offense, because we never had a goal-line situation. See, Buddy? This guy wasn't a wasted draft choice.

We beat the Vikings pretty easily 27–9. We were 8–0 and cooking.

Looking at the old papers, I see that really dumb-ass Dunkel thing. Even a stupid Dunkel can figure stuff out eventually. At last we were rated No. 1 in the NFL. Took them long enough to figure it out.

But now it was Packer week again, and we were going up to Green Bay. This wasn't Soldier Field tailgating. There weren't going to be Bears fans anywhere. There was a lot of mouthiness going on already, especially, it seemed to me, from their side. They were only 3–5, but the Packers-Bears series is

like a division within the division. Lose to them, and it diminishes anything else you accomplish.

Like I said, I didn't hate the Packers. When I went up there as a rookie coach in 1982, they had one of the classiest guys I'd ever met in my life at coach, Bart Starr. I had great respect for him, both as a player and a leader. Here it is, my first game, and they put on the Lambeau scoreboard, "THE GREEN BAY PACKERS WELCOME MIKE DITKA AND THE CHICAGO BEARS." They didn't have to do that. Everybody was saying this is hostile country, but that was just classy.

I wasn't so sure now. Maybe they were still mad about Fridge running over them. Maybe George Cumby represented the little guys who get in the way of a concrete mixer. I don't know, but the Packers came out and were dirtier than dirt. It was disgusting. Just a few minutes into the game this defensive back named Mark Lee hit Payton after Walter was already out of bounds and knocked him into the wall beyond the bench. What the hell was that? They threw Lee out of the game. And it only fired up Walter. The guy had over 100 yards rushing by halftime. He had 192 yards for the game, his most in eight years. But this was just chickenshit. I was so angry I could have busted my clipboard into sawdust. Packers players had towels with hit lists on them. They absolutely did.

Some clown named Ken Stills had already hit McMahon late and hard. Then he came flying up from I don't know how far away and creamed Suhey from the blind side three or four seconds after a play was over. Suhey was a tough kid, but he could have been really hurt bad. Stills got a 15-yard penalty, but he should have been thrown out of the game, too. It was the most gutless move I think I've ever seen, because if he'd done it straight, Matt would've kicked his ass from here to next year. And if Stills was told to do it by his coach, his coach is gutless, too.

It was ugly. I might have told my team to retaliate, but I'm not sure if I did. Anyway, they didn't. We just played football. That's all you can do. I think even a lot of Packers fans were embarrassed by the actions of some of their players. Those actions were horrendous. They stunk. It was the ultimate cowardliness that I'd ever seen on a field. It was so contrary to everything the Packers stood for. This might have been the only time there was actual hatred between the teams. And I maintain to this day that it was instigated by one man, their coach. If you can't control your team, then it's your fault. The league didn't fine guys back then like they do now, or that might have got the players' attention, since Forrest Gregg sure didn't. There might have been some of the biggest fines ever given in sports. Walter said after the game he thought Lee was a guy trying to impress his coach. And he probably was.

The reason the Packers were doing all of this

was because they weren't good enough to line up against us nose to nose and beat us. In 1983 we were playing the Detroit Lions and they had us basically beaten, and then they faked a field goal and threw a touchdown pass to pile it on. I was hot. I got Dave Duerson, who was a rookie, and told him that on the kickoff I didn't care what happened, I wanted him to knock Lions kicker Eddie Murray on his ass. Maybe some players wouldn't have done it, but Dave did. He knocked the crap out of Murray. Just blasted him. The Detroit coaches were out of their minds, screaming at us, yelling to the refs. It was legal. They're all wearing pads. Just because he's a kicker doesn't mean he can't get hit. But maybe it wasn't right.

Anyway, I was young and madder than they were. But Murray never talked to me again. I used to play in some golf tournaments, and he'd be there and would just turn the other way.

Detroit's coach back then was Monte Clark, and I know he was a good guy. The problem was mine. It was basically me not knowing what it took to be a mature, solid head coach. We played the Seahawks in 1982 when I was a rookie coach, and they ran a triple reverse on us for big yardage, and the press asked me about it afterward. I said it was a stupid-ass high school play. That was wrong, too. I had no reason to say that. I learned that the other guys are always going to remember what you said. And if you'll notice, after a couple years, I never gave the opponent any more bulletin-board material. I never said a word.

In the Green Bay game, not that I was trying to make a point or anything, but I sent William Perry in for a play just before half. We were down 3–0 at the time, and I knew the Packers thought Fridge was going to steamroll somebody, probably Cumby, all over again. We put William in motion to the right—he looked like a sumo wrestler heading for the ring—and then he slid along the line of scrimmage toward the end zone. The defender had braced for a collision, but Fridge went past him, and McMahon threw him a perfect pass for a four-yard touchdown. Perry caught it with his hands like it was a basketball, his hands reversed from the way football receivers do it, and walked in untouched. Gregg had to be furious. That put us ahead 7–3, and we hung on to win 16–10. I'm not sure, but I think McMahon gave Forrest the finger as he ran off for halftime. Sorry about that.

Some Chicago writer called Perry the "Galloping Roast," and Gary Fencik said what was true: using Perry as a threat was funny, but "he has to be taken seriously." Damn right. I refuse to make it all drudgery. I just don't believe in that. But the fun is effective. Why shouldn't it be? I look at all of these coaches nowadays and you see them in press conferences and, hell, you can't figure out if they won or lost. Does his wife love him or did she just divorce his sorry ass? Mr. Blankface, what's your problem? It's like all of you guys have been cloned. HAVE SOME FUN!

The papers called Fridge the Galloping Roast? At least they didn't say he was the "Stuffed Turkey." I told you how amazing it was to see him on this diet in later years and him working so hard in practice and still not losing weight. Of course, I found out they were bringing pizzas and cases of beer into the dorm late at night, and he'd be wolfing the stuff down—I think he could drink a case of beer no problem—and then he'd be five pounds heavier at weigh-ins the next morning. And he couldn't figure out why his diet wasn't working.

The thing is, sports are a one-time thing. You better do what you can when you can do it. Maybe you can be a doctor for 50 years, or drive a truck that long, but your sports career comes and goes in a hurry. I heard from somebody later in the season that Michael Jordan had broken his foot and had already been out for weeks. And there he was just starting his second year with the Bulls after an unbelievable rookie season. He was probably out for a long time. You never know. That's why this was so important. Right now. This season. This week. This practice. This play.

So far, so good.

We had been forced to come from behind six times, but we were still undefeated. And we were halfway to our goal. ∎

Chicago 27, Minnesota 9
Every Phase Earns Praise

The Bears did not put themselves in another hole against Minnesota and need to turn to Jim McMahon, as they had in Game 3. This time they put away the Vikings early and kept them down in what some thought was one of their best games of the season.

McMahon struck with a 33-yard touchdown pass to Dennis McKinnon in the first quarter, and Kevin Butler made it 10–0 with a 40-yard field goal. Minnesota fought back with a one-yard touchdown run by Darrin Nelson, but another Butler field goal put the Bears up 13–7 at halftime.

The Minnesota offense was done for the most part after that first score. The Bears' defense went on an interception frenzy against Tommy Kramer, the Minnesota quarterback who had been so effec-tive against them in the first meeting, and backup Wade Wilson. The Bears' five interceptions gave them 21 through eight games, the same number they'd had for all of 1984. In fact, Otis Wilson returned one interception 23 yards for a touch-down in the third quarter.

The game marked the first real appearance of William Perry at defensive tackle. He recorded his first NFL sack and played well enough to be inserted into the starting lineup for the final eight games of the season. For all the attention paid to his time as a running or blocking back, this was the job he most wanted to do.

While the defense was holding the Vikings to 30 rushing yards, the Bears were getting Walter Payton 118 yards on 19 carries and 202 rushing

Otis Wilson leads the cheers after a fourth-quarter sack of the Vikings' Tommy Kramer.

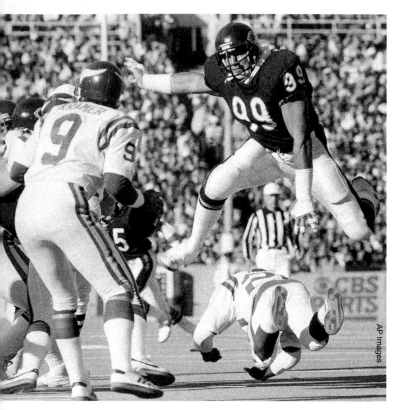

AP Images

gained on offense and fewest allowed on defense.

The offense was continuing to stretch out in its distribution of the ball among backs, wide receivers, and tight ends. Payton and Matt Suhey each caught five passes, Emery Moorehead four, Tim Wrightman two, and McKinnon, Willie Gault, and James Maness one apiece. ■

Chicago 27, Minnesota 9
OCT. 27, 1985, AT SOLDIER FIELD

BOTTOM LINE

Five picked-off passes knock Vikes for loop

KEY PLAY
Otis Wilson's 23-yard interception return for a touchdown. It squelched a Minnesota rally and gave the Bears room to breathe at 20–7.

KEY STAT
The Bears stuffed Vikings' running game, allowing only 30 yards.

yards as a team. This was Payton's third straight 100-yard game in what would be a record-setting stretch of 100-yarders.

The Bears amassed 413 yards of total offense, the fourth time in eight games they had topped 400 yards. At the midpoint of the season they were the NFL's only undefeated team and led in yards

Chicago Bears tackle Dan Hampton leaps over a downed Minnesota Viking to corner quarterback Tommy Kramer during the game in Chicago on October 28, 1985 (above). Mike Hartenstine helps Wilber Marshall to his feet after a Kevin Butler field goal (right).

RICHARD DENT

No. 95, defensive end

"The championship game with the Rams, seeing the snow coming down, the guys are happy because you know you're going to the Super Bowl. To be at home and feel the enjoyment that was taking place was awesome."

"I'm sure the Patriots knew it was over before they got there."

"In certain formations and certain things they would get into, myself or Mike [Singletary] or [Dan] Hampton would call that play out, and you'd see their guys looking at each other."

"I think Mike Ditka always kept us on the edge. He had ways of getting us ready. Some of the things, we didn't see eye to eye on—some of the ways in trying to motivate me that I didn't appreciate. But outside of that, we had a good time."

"Buddy [Ryan] put the game in our hands. He put the game plan in our hands. You don't see that much today. You see it maybe with Peyton Manning. You see it mostly on the offensive side. You don't see it on the defensive side."

"You think about things like not letting teams score, negative yards at halftime—you just don't see that. Some of the things we did, you just don't see. And the point of it was that you shared some things with some guys that were very rare."

"The way people look at us and this particular team—how much we won, how well we played, how well we entertained people—people think we won three, four Super Bowls. We had that caliber of team. We tampered with the quarterback position a lot."

"I thought we should've won more Super Bowls. We lost a couple opportunities there with [Doug] Flutie."

"I'm an eighth-rounder, and when you're drafted in that position, you're there for a couple years until they find something better. In this case, they found something great."

"You're trying to figure out a guy's weakness, and what I would do is work on his weakness. In

your eyes, you think I'm taking a play off. But you don't understand the game, so you wouldn't know what I'm doing. I spend my week working on things where a guy's weak."

———————

"I guess when I was growing up I always wanted to be someone in my community that people looked up to. I had dreams of a Super Bowl team, Super Bowl MVP, all the things that I accomplished. Yes, I had dreams of that.

"If you don't know how to commit yourself, then you aren't going to be anything."

———————

"I guess I'm a people watcher. I enjoy seeing people accomplish dreams and things of that nature. I remember meeting Venus Williams back in '87, '88. Watching people go from nowhere to get to somewhere. Because I know I've kind of done the same thing. I had the chance to crawl out from under a rock, from nowhere to become something." ■

chapter X

Howling Sounds and Defenders from Another Planet

After the Packers game Walter Payton had danced past reporters, saying, reminiscent of the old Jackie Gleason Honeymooners line, "Nine-and-oh, and away we go!"

The Bears were definitely in high gear. Except, of course, for Jim McMahon, who was dealing with leaking tires and busted gaskets. Now his right shoulder was sprained. In practice early in the week, he threw left-handed. Not well, but he threw. But he could barely lift his right arm and had been told by trainer Fred Caito not to use it. Jimmy Mac grinned his twisted grin and said, "I enjoy pain." It was a good marriage, then. But as the days before the Detroit Lions game passed, it became clearer that McMahon was not going to be fit to play, perhaps for a while.

Also mixed into that week was the finding on Thursday in Schaumburg Circuit Court of a guilty verdict for Ditka of driving under the influence after the 49ers game. Ditka was subdued and reasonable in court. His attorney, Don Reuben, complained that Ditka had been handcuffed "and trussed like a chicken." Asked by judge Earl B. Hoffenberg if his client had been abusive toward the arresting officer, Reuben replied, "I suspect anyone would be cantankerous if they were handcuffed."

"McMichael was like a Harley-Davidson biker. Singletary was like a minister." —Ditka

"You are a well-known public figure," the judge said to Ditka. "You have a great deal of influence over young adults."

The coach nodded, saying he had been speaking to young people about responsible driving for some time. He was sentenced to a year of court supervision, fined $300, and ordered to attend at least 10 hours of driving school. Basically, he needed to do his penance, and steer clear of further arrests, and matters would work out fine.

I still thought I wasn't guilty. I had only been clocked at 63 in a 55-mph zone, and there were cars going past me at 95. Go 55, and you'll get killed. But that was 25 years ago, and I'm not mad at anyone. The judge made his decision, and that's that. It was very embarrassing for me; to the Bears; to Jerry Vainisi, who's my friend; to the players; and to my family. But I didn't lose authority with the team. And I think that is because they realized I was just a regular guy who had made a mistake.

And now I knew that McMahon was definitely out. There wouldn't be any off-the-bench heroics like in the first Vikings game. Steve Fuller had to play, and he hadn't started since that first Minnesota game. He's a good guy, and

he handled the way he got yanked very well.

There was pressure on us now, because we were everybody's target. But what I remember is how windy it was going into that game. It was mid-November, and it was cold and wet, but mostly it was incredibly windy. I watched warmups before the game, and the wind was roaring out of the north like crazy. The flags looked like they were hooked to airplanes. Passes went everywhere. Sid Luckman couldn't have thrown in that wind.

So I decided to run the ball. The first 21 plays I called were runs. Maybe that was overdoing it. Yeah, it was overdoing it. Hell, for the game we ran 55 times! But I was starting to get a little tight, and I didn't want a game like this to slip away because of interceptions or stuff that was almost accidental. I knew this was how I lost the 49ers game in the playoffs last year, by being too conservative, but I didn't want mistakes to be the reason the Lions won. Payton and Suhey both rushed for over 100 yards. I guess inside I knew the Lions weren't that good. They couldn't stop us, and we won 24–3.

The only time I used Fridge on offense, he went in motion again, like that pass play. But Fuller snuck it in from the 1 for a touchdown. Perry was definitely a big deal, though. On Monday he went to New York to be on *Letterman*. He had his front tooth out, as always, but he had a coat and tie and sweater vest on, and he looked nice. Letterman asked him if it was true he had once drunk 48 beers after a Clemson victory over North Carolina. Fridge nodded and said, "It was a big game."

The thing is a team consists of a lot of different people. Steve McMichael and Mike Singletary were both from Texas, but after that they were about as different as two people could be. McMichael was like a Harley-Davidson biker. Singletary was like a minister. I think he might have been a minister, might have actually had ministry papers. I don't think they ever had a conversation that lasted more than seven seconds. So what? They respected each other. And they both had huge hearts.

We didn't have the NFL combine back in those days, thank God, because neither of them would have impressed anybody at an idiotic meat market like that. Singletary, I mean, he's in the Hall of Fame and I think he's on his way to being a terrific NFL coach. He had a great study and work ethic, and he was intelligent. And he had discipline. But he was short and he wore glasses, and how do you think he would have rated in the computers? Those combines are unadulterated bullshit. You go to Indianapolis and watch somebody run 40s and lift weights and jump around, and you think you can tell me he's going to be a great football player? IQ tests are nothing. How many times

do they hand you pencils out on the field?

When I came out of college, it was even more primitive. In my rookie training camp Halas said he wanted me to run a 40.

I said, "Why?"

He said, "I just want you to run it."

So I did. And I ran a 4.7 on grass, maybe like a 4.73, which surprised me. That's pretty good. Of course, it was before I dislocated my foot. But I knew I could run. I knew it my whole life, from when I was a kid and I ran everywhere. That's what you do. There were guys who were fast as hell, but I watched Walter Payton run, and I watched Barry Sanders run, and they weren't all that fast. But I never saw people catching them from behind.

There were true sprinters like Bob Hayes and my onetime roommate Johnny Morris, who had some short indoor record like the 50-yard dash or something. But I saw Willie Galimore beat him by five yards in a 40. Willie, man, he could fly. And so could his buddy, Johnny Farrington. They were as exciting as it gets. They were Bears teammates of mine back in the early days. Galimore was a back out of Florida A&M, and he ran for 181 yards in a game my second year. Farrington, whose nickname was Bo, was a wide receiver from Prairie View, and he still holds the Bears' longest reception record, 98 yards.

They were on our 1963 championship team, and we should have had a great team in 1964. But one night at preseason training camp down in Rensselaer, Indiana, in August 1964, Willie and Bo went to a country club bar to watch the Olympics on TV and maybe have a beer or two. It was an off-day and they were coming back on this twisting highway that led to camp. The mowers had just cut the grass, and I think they took down some signs that pointed out the curves. Willie was driving, and he went off the road and then swerved to get back on, and one of the wheels evidently collapsed

your chance, and it's why you shouldn't let the trivial things make you crazy. Way back, I was ridiculous. Are you kidding me? It got to the point where it was beyond stupidity, with my anger and all. Like with Harbaugh on the sideline, even then I was 500 times wrong, but I was so pissed off about that audible I wanted to kill him. Same with Avellini. Why? Why couldn't I just pat him on the back and say, "Don't do it again"?

Maybe it came from just wanting to win so

"My high school coach said, 'You should study dentistry. You can be a dentist and come back here and make great money.' Sounded good to me."

—Ditka

and the car rolled. It was a Volkswagen with the top open, and Willie flew out the roof and was killed, and then the car rolled over and broke Johnny's neck and killed him.

I was 24 years old, and the next morning I went down to the morgue with my teammates Rick Casares and Bill George, and I looked at the bodies on the slab. There was not one mark on Willie, not one mark. And Farrington had a cut on his face.

It was devastating to me. It was devastating to the team. We should have been really good in 1964, but we went 5–9, and it was like our soul had been cut out. I know we're all going to die. That's why you have to try hard when you've got

bad. Back when I was in Little League in Aliquippa, I'd be pitching, and a teammate would make an error, and I'd get so mad I'd tell the manager I wanted to play that position and to bring in another pitcher. I was nuts. But I just think that winning is important. Because if you line up in life and you accept defeat, then you will be defeated. And you'll get what you were ready for. When you quit, you're defeated. Right there. That's the equation. If you keep fighting, you've got a chance.

Look, you can't say you're going to be the greatest in everything. Take singing, for instance. You want to sing like Sinatra? We have a singer here at my restaurant on Chestnut Street who is very good, John Vincent, who sounds a hell of a lot like Frank. But in fourth grade the nun told me, "Michael, it sounds like you're howling. Do NOT sing." So I wasn't going anywhere with my voice. I will not be singing here at my upstairs bar, for instance.

Do we pick the things we're good at, or do they pick us? I'm not sure it matters. When I was a kid, I was a pretty good baseball player. I had a big strike zone, but if I got hold of it, it went. I played at Pitt, and one game we played against Kent State, and they had a pitcher who ended up with the Yankees. He put one down the middle and, man, I blasted it way over the centerfield wall. It was big time. Tommy Lasorda scouted me, and years later he said, "You had a big strike zone, but I watched you hit one way over the fence."

I had a chance to sign a minor league contract. But I wanted to go to college and get an education, even though I had no idea what that really meant or what it would be in. My high school coach said, "You should study dentistry. You can be a dentist and come back here and make great money." Sounded good to me.

So you get into the what-ifs. What if I had gone to Pitt and blown out my knee, and that was it for sports? I guess I would have come back to Aliquippa and worked in the steel mill. The dentistry thing wouldn't have happened. I mean, think of Dr. Ditka. Me looking in people's mouths? I think I'd rather knock teeth out than put them in. But you don't know. Maybe I wouldn't have quit school; maybe I

would have become that dentist. And a good one. A nice, sweet dentist. The point is, my life wouldn't have ended. What would have happened if I'd gotten hurt? I never really have thought about it. None of that "Why me, not him?" stuff. I played with a lot of guys from all over the state of Pennsylvania, tough kids, and they hurt a knee or whatever and were never the same. It's a risk, but you don't think about it. Back then, you hurt your knee, it was like butchery—they put your leg in a huge cast, and your career could be finished.

At Pitt we came in with a hardnosed freshman class, and I remember in one scrimmage we kicked the shit out of the varsity. Because we wanted it bad. There's fate involved in life, but I don't think the key to life is chance. It's when you realize what an opportunity you have, and you snatch it. I got a chance to play football and a chance to coach it, and that was enough for me. I made up my mind a long time ago that eventually I would coach the Chicago Bears. I didn't know how it would happen. There was a lot of dumb stuff along the way. I had to grow up. I left Chicago on bad terms with Mr. Halas. And then at the end, in 1992, I was terminated by the powers that be. That was 100 percent jealousy. One McCaskey at the top was never thrilled with me, and now he wanted everything for himself. So it goes.

But what I could always come back to was this: I'd been drafted by the man who started the NFL. And the man who started it had asked me to coach. That's a pretty close connection to the roots of football. Not like being the pope, but it was pretty good.

Now we had the Dallas Cowboys coming up. Halas may have given me more opportunities than anyone else, but nobody flat-out helped me more than Cowboys coach Tom Landry. It was almost like we were going from Forrest Gregg, who was Darth Vader, to Moses.

Everybody needs help in life. When you come to the Y in the road, you have to take one way or the other. When I came to the Y, Coach Landry was standing there, and he said, "Come this way." And I went that way, and that's basically that. He believed I could be a coach. I know he was worried that if I couldn't control myself, how could I control others? But he let me work on that.

The main thing he told me when I finally got the Bears job was, "Whether you succeed or not, do it your way. Don't ever leave yourself open to doing it somebody else's way and then blame them if you fail." That was wonderful advice, because at the beginning I did listen to everybody. Who doesn't? Tom was more important to me than anyone in a way, even more than my dad. I had a great high school coach. And Coach Halas was my coach as a football player. But Tom was my coach as a coach.

I basically brought his offense to the Bears. I changed a few things, but I even numbered the holes the way he did, which was very unusual. We had the odd numbers—1, 3, 5, 7, 9—to the right, and the even—2, 4, 6, 8—to the left. Everybody in football does it the opposite way, but not in Dallas. I think Tom did it that way because he was looking at it from the defensive standpoint, seeing it from their eyes. I did it his way. I couldn't change it.

I know people said we were about as different as two people could be, him so stoic and calm and me all keyed-up. But I looked up to him. And I think he saw something in me he respected and appreciated, and maybe he even was a little like me. He knew, no matter what, how much I cared about the game and doing things well. I'd been his player and then his assistant, and now that I was an NFL head coach, we still talked all the time. I needed his advice on so many things. I could call, and he would always be there for me. He was my biggest booster.

So now we have to play his team, the Cowboys, "America's Team," down in Dallas. And they're pretty good, as they always were under Tom. They're 7–3 and in first place in the NFC East. This was another big test for us. We got past the Redskins and the 49ers and the Packers, twice. And we had the undefeated streak. But Dallas is Dallas. They beat us last year, the only time we'd played them since I started coaching the Bears. We were only favored by a point.

McMahon was definitely out; his shoulder tendinitis wasn't improving, so Fuller was my guy again. Good old Steve. I loved him to death. But was he up to this? And I didn't know how I felt for sure about this contest. I was the pupil going against the teacher. I had a lot of emotions going around. Believe me, I was pretty chewed up inside.

And then we played. And we annihilated Dallas. Buddy's philosophy was simple: "Take the sum-bitch away from them in a hurry." Meaning the ball. Our defense mutilated the Cowboys. It became like a snowball going downhill. Those poor Dallas quarterbacks didn't know whether to shit or go blind. I can still see their backup quarterback Gary Hogeboom, when he was already on his way to the turf, and Singletary hit him so hard before he could reach the ground that I thought Mike had killed him.

The offense was solid. We gained almost 400 yards, and Payton had another 100-yard day. But the defense shut everything down. Richard Dent caught a pass tipped by Hampton at the goal line and ran it in for a touchdown. Cornerback Mike Richardson ran an interception back for a score. Les Frazier had a long interception return. Otis Wilson knocked their starting quarterback, Danny White, out of the game. Twice. Jeez, I started to feel sorry for White, down on the turf, his helmet off, half-conscious. Our defense was crazy, like attack dogs, and they started barking. "Woof! Woof!"

Somewhere in the third quarter I said to Buddy, "Can you slow these guys down?"

And he said, "Mike, I can't."

Our defense was gone. On another planet.

We won 44–0 with a backup quarterback. It was the worst loss for Dallas, ever. By the end Texas Stadium was silent, except for all of the Bears fans, who were barking and singing.

I felt good, but I also felt bad. Here we were, doing what we could only dream about doing. And yet it was the worst thing, too. We had our picture taken before the game, Coach Landry and me, our arms around each other. This was the guy I'd learned everything from. He was a good racquetball player, and when I was coaching under him, he and I and Dan Reeves and Ernie Stautner and a bunch of guys would play after practice. We had fun, and then he'd say, "Go home. Be with your families. If we can't get our work done during the day, something's wrong." He never asked the assistants to stay real late. He taught me that sometimes you overthink things, you try to change game plans so much that you're just messing with something that isn't broken. There was probably nothing he was prouder of than when Dan Reeves and I both became head coaches after studying under him.

But 44–0?

In life there are conflicts like that. It hurt. But I remember just a week before I'd been watching *Monday Night Football,* and Redskins quarterback Joe Theismann got hit by Lawrence Taylor, and his leg broke in half. Compound fracture. They caught it on tape. And it made me sick. Theismann never played another down of football.

But that was life. Life went on.

And now I wanted to go without a loss, ever. ■

Chicago 16, Green Bay 10
Circus Stars: Perry, Payton

Six personal fouls in the first half and a horde of cheap shots might have made it a pro wrestling match. William Perry's first touchdown catch might have made it a circus. Instead, Walter Payton turned the Bears' ninth straight victory into a personal tour de force. He matched the third-best performance of his career by rushing for 192 yards and sealed the Bears' closest victory of the season with a 27-yard touchdown run in the fourth quarter.

Payton's winning score came on an audible. Coach Mike Ditka had called for a pass to Payton to the left side, but when Jim McMahon saw the defense stacked, he changed the play to a run behind tackle Keith Van Horne on the right. Payton cut through the line, broke a tackle at the 20-yard line and outran the Green Bay secondary to the end zone. It was his 13th 100-yard performance in 20 games against the Packers, the 68th 100-yard game of his career, and his fourth in a row.

Payton's heroics were preceded by Perry's debut as a receiver. Trailing 3–0 early in the second quarter, the Bears sent Perry into the backfield. Payton had to tell him where to line up before the Refrigerator put his 308 pounds into slow motion toward the flat. Two weeks earlier, Perry had blasted Green Bay linebacker George Cumby into the end zone. This time Cumby was the victim again.

"They saw him coming and got out of the way," Ditka said.

Having been humiliated two weeks earlier in a

William Perry grabs a four-yard touchdown pass during the Bears' victory at Lambeau Field.

safety Dave Duerson acknowledged, "Let's face it. It wasn't clean on either side."

When the Bears arrived at their Lambeau Field locker room before the game, they found a bag of fertilizer from a Wisconsin radio station with the note: "Here's what you guys are full of." Payton aside, that might have been an appropriate odor for this game. ■

Chicago 16, Green Bay 10
NOV. 3, 1985, AT LAMBEAU FIELD

BOTTOM LINE
Packers bamboozled in contentious game

KEY PLAY Walter Payton's 27-yard
touchdown run. It clinched the victory and kept the Bears undefeated.

KEY STAT
Payton ran for 192 yards on 28 carries.

Monday night loss featuring Perry's first TD run, the Packers decided to get down and, especially, dirty. Tempers flared repeatedly. Green Bay cornerback Mark Lee was ejected after he ran Payton out of bounds and completely over the bench. After another play had wound down, Packers safety Ken Stills leveled McMahon. Even so, Bears

Walter Payton ends up in a bear hug from tackle Jim Covert after scoring on a 27-yard run (right), and Steve McMichael gets his arms around the legs of Green Bay quarterback Jim Zorn (above).

WILLIE GAULT

No. 83, wide receiver

"'The Super Bowl Shuffle' came about when I was doing another video with Sister Sledge. From that, the producer of that video, Linda Clifford, we started talking and we said we should do a Bears video. I think it was a really gutsy thing that we did. It was revolutionary. Historic. I think it was part of who we were. It fit us perfectly because we were a team that was very confident."

"46–10. 'The Super Bowl Shuffle.' Walter Payton. The Fridge. McMahon's headband. Richard Dent, MVP. Amazing defense. It's a magical moment that will never be lived again. So you look at those moments and you cherish them."

"We had people coming from Russia, Germany, Japan, everywhere, watching our practice. We were arguably one of the most popular teams in the history of the NFL."

"I don't think there was a better coach for our team that year. I think Mike Ditka exemplified what the Bears were all about—the way he played, his tenacity. That's the same way he coached. Buddy Ryan, same thing."

"Walter was a mentor. When I first came to camp as a rookie, he was one of the first persons to greet me. He gave me a hug and almost squeezed the breath out of me."

"See, here's the thing with me: I know who I am. I don't really need someone to validate me to tell me who I am. I know who I am."

"I would go into Mayor Washington's office and we would talk about the city, life, people, the Bears and all that. We had a special relationship."

"My mom and dad were probably some of my best friends. They were friends, but yet they were disciplinarians. They taught me right from wrong. They let me make decisions in my life very early. But they gave me tools to make those decisions."

"I had good friends and good enemies. Good enemies are the ones who tell you you're not going to do anything or be anything, and in your mind you go, 'I'll prove it.'"

"I knew that I was the fastest guy on the field."

"I took more hits than anybody could imagine. I have all my catches on one reel—catches and being thrown to, all of it—and I got hit a lot. It's a contact sport. People think I didn't like it, but the object of a receiver is not to get hit. You want to try to catch the ball and try to make a touchdown."

"The ballet was an opportunity to help save

the Chicago City Ballet, which I'd never done before, but I thought it would be worthwhile saving."

"If I live my life based on opinions and what people say and think, then I would be a really sad person. Be your own man. Be a leader, not a follower. That's the main thing." ■

chapter XI

Traveling South, Near-Blows with Buddy, *Monday Night* Hell

The Bears horse-whipped the lowly Atlanta Falcons 36–0 the next week. It was more of the same. More defense. More Payton. More McMahon still out with injuries—mainly that bad shoulder. Indeed, rumors from Halas Hall were that McMahon might be done for the season. The Fridge got himself an airborne one-yard touchdown dive in the blowout, a move he said he copied after further studying Payton's leaping heroics. According to the Sun-Times, Perry's self-launch to paydirt "alarmed both air traffic controllers and earthquake monitors."

Ditka was amused and a little awestruck himself by the carnage. "They must have felt like it was Sherman's army marching through them," he said of the Atlantans. Even third-string Bears quarterback Mike Tomczak got some quality minutes in the rout.

"I used to play the game, and I remembered what it was like when the Old Man fined me. That really bothered me!" —Ditka on fining McMahon

The Bears were playing at a level never seen in the NFL. The "46" defense looked like a single wave of attackers storming a straw hut. Mike Singletary was outraged when he learned Atlanta running back Gerald Riggs had gained 100 yards, the first 100-yard game given up by the defense since the opener against Tampa Bay, when James Wilder got 166. "You have to understand Mike," Ditka said. "And his pride."

Now the obvious challenge for the Bears was to go without a loss. Standing in the way of the 12–0 team was this week's opponent, the Miami Dolphins. The game was to be at the Orange Bowl, the Dolphins' home field, where coach Don Shula and his young genius quarterback Dan Marino ruled. Indeed, the Dolphins had won 17 of their last 18 games in the always-jammed, old-fashioned, humid and palm tree-dotted arena. It was a fitting matchup, because it was Shula's 1972 Dolphins who were the only team in NFL history to go undefeated, including winning the Super Bowl. That 1972 team had a curious parallel to the Bears' 1985 team in that in the previous season the Dolphins had marched all of the way to the Super Bowl, only to lose. Those 1971 Dolphins had lost 24–3 to the Dallas Cowboys, who featured a tight end named Mike Ditka.

"We got beat, and we didn't like it," then-Miami quarterback Bob Griese said later. "So really our season started with a loss the year before." Same with the Bears. Their 23–0 spanking in the 1984 NFC Championship Game had festered badly. At the end of the Bears' 44–0 demolition of the Cowboys two weeks earlier, inflamed and single-minded middle-linebacker/preacher Mike Singletary had turned to the Texas crowd and screamed, "Don't leave! I want witnesses!"

Going undefeated in the NFL wasn't just hard. It was a transcendent goal; maybe, with the extended schedule, impossible. The 1972 Dolphins had finished 17–0. Prior to Super Bowl play, NFL teams only played a maximum of 13 games, final game included. Now the Bears would have to go 19–0—16 regular-season wins and three playoff wins—to achieve perfection. That didn't stop Bears analysts from crowing. A headline above Sun-Times football writer Kevin Lamb's column said, "If Stats Don't Lie, It's Bears By 40."

Stats weren't going to mean much in this face-off on national TV, again an ABC Monday Night spectacular. This would be about intangibles, luck, bounces. The Bears were well on their way to being the first team since those undefeated 1972 Dolphins to lead the NFL in points scored and fewest points allowed. They were ahead of everyone by 40 offensively and 45 defensively. In the last four games they had outscored their opponents 120–13. The average score of their last three games—all quarterbacked by Steve Fuller—was a ridiculous, 35–1. Still…

The contest would be the highest rated for Monday Night Football, ever. Even to this day. Everybody tuned in to see the battle, to see these barking dogs, this high-wire act, this invading horde, and the obstacle in front of them.

McMahon is still hurt, but I'm used to it now. He makes a crack about how he needs to play so he can make some money on his incentives, so he can pay all the fines I've laid on him. I don't know about that. If I fined anybody that year, it was minimal. Really minimal. I had rules, but they weren't much. I probably had a double standard for some guys. But I don't remember fining many guys that year. I hated to take their money. I used to play the game, and I remembered what it was like when the Old Man fined me. That really bothered me! In retrospect, yeah, I deserved it. But it pissed me off.

In a sense, there's no question I was too compassionate toward the players. Not the coaches, maybe…but the players. I know later on I kept guys too long, after they were done. But I couldn't help it. I always remembered being a player, how your life was in the hands of the coach.

We're traveling to Miami and not much of this is on my mind, because all I'm thinking of is what a great coach Don Shula is and what a great passer Marino is. Still, I knew we had a team that was incredible.

We get to the Orange Bowl, and the crowd is at a fever pitch. That's fine. Cops have German Shepherds on leashes. We're used to noise and craziness by now. It was humid but not hot, because this is already the beginning of December. Somebody has told me we've lost our last eight *Monday Night* games when we're on the road. Yeah? Screw 'em. Screw those statistics, all of it. This isn't a pinball game. This is football.

But something is wrong with this night. The Dolphins are having Marino roll away from Dent, which is smart, but we can't get to him with the other guys. They're using little wide receiver Nat Moore like a tight end, putting him in the slot and putting him in motion. We've seen three-receiver sets, but this has three wideouts and no true tight

The '85 Bears

end. So we have to cover Moore with a linebacker like Wilbur Marshall or, after a while, we moved Fencik up in man-to-man, but he's more of a deep safety, and that's not a good matchup, either.

Now, Dent is an impact player. He should be in the Hall of Fame, no question about it. He was the 203rd player taken in the 1983 draft out of dinky Tennessee State, and he was skinny and raw and hadn't played against anybody. But he worked his ass off, bulked up, used his athleticism. I kidded him, calling him Robert, but that was just because he wanted more money, more publicity, and I was messing with him. But he was the real deal, a great pass-rushing defensive end.

Thing was, in this game Marino stayed away from him. Marino did his half-rollouts to stay away, and he had that quick release. A quick-draw gunslinger's gun. The problem is, Dent can't do anything, because he's got to go 15 yards or more to get to Marino, and we're asking our linebackers, guys who are used to going straight ahead, to drop back in coverage. We should have gone to a nickel. Five defensive backs. They're running what is essentially a third-down-and-long formation a whole lot of the time. They hadn't shown that before. Not throughout an entire game. And we didn't adjust. Sure, it was more complicated than that, but that was at the root of it.

Steve Fuller was doing what he could on offense. He never worried about his limitations, he never worried about being a star, about notoriety, none of it. He was a true team player, and he had confidence, because he'd had early success with the Kansas City Chiefs. He planned and prepared like nobody else. He was very smart—he was a Rhodes Scholar candidate at Clemson—and he's made a great success in real estate down in South Carolina since his football career ended. I never looked at him as just a backup, but, still, it was McMahon, the rebel grenade, who could do the genius things. And he was on the bench.

Miami got lucky, too. They blocked a punt by Maury Buford and recovered it at our 6. They even had a horseshit pass that Hampton deflected, and it should have been intercepted, but it went way up in the air, and damned if their toothpick wideout Mark Clayton didn't catch it for a long score. But that wasn't what pissed me off.

No, I was mad at Buddy. Look, what we're doing on defense isn't working. So let's adapt! Wilbur Marshall is one of the best athletes I've seen, but don't ask him to cover wide receivers 30 yards downfield. We should have gone to a straight nickel. Rush four linemen, use two linebackers, and have the five DBs cover. Maybe the problem was who do you take out? It might have hurt somebody's ego. Maybe Buddy's. Otis Wilson is a good linebacker, but why didn't we put Reggie Phillips in there in the nickel? If you're not flexible to make adjustments, to change what's not working, you'll never win. The "46" had been ungodly up until this game. But we needed to fine-tune it. Right now! You have to give your players the best chance to win. You can't handicap them. If the tanks are getting blown up, come in with the Air Force. That's all I was saying.

So we come in at halftime, down 31–10. We've given up more points in two quarters than we had in the last six entire games! Goddamn, I was furious. Later, people would say I was doing too much off-field stuff, commercials and TV shows and what have you, that I wasn't paying attention to the store. That was bull. My mind was always on the goal.

I go up to Buddy and I start screaming at him. "What are you doing out there? We have to run the nickel! Let's blitz the shit out of them!" He yells back at me, and now we've got a pissing match. We're pushing and yelling, and the players are there, and it's not a good thing. It's pretty ugly. Players separate us, and we move apart. I try to calm down. Football is a tense game. I've seen two assistants go at it. But not a head coach and a coordinator. All I'm trying to get across is that you don't let your men get beat just because you won't combat what the other side is doing. I'll go to my grave believing that.

I think Buddy and I resolved the conflict before the half ended. And I think I apologized to him after the game. At any rate, Fuller got hurt in the fourth quarter, so I put McMahon in the game, hoping that maybe he could do stuff just like in that first Minnesota game. But it wasn't there. He had no magic under his hat. He got sacked a couple times and threw an interception. We lost 38–24, and it stunk.

The only good thing that happened was I kept Walter in at the end, handing him the ball so he could get 100 yards. He got 121, his eighth straight 100-yard game, an NFL record. I wanted him to beat that *Monday Night* TV guy, O.J. Simpson, who had been tied with him at seven. Simpson was always second-guessing us. So now he could second-guess Payton's record.

They told me Fridge's new McDonald's ad had debuted at halftime of the *Monday Night* game. Swell.

Nobody is invincible. And nobody that season was undefeated. Not even us, the mighty Bears.

We had to regroup. ■

Chicago 24, Detroit 3
Against Fuller, Lions on Empty

Jim McMahon sat this one out with tendinitis in his right shoulder, but Steve Fuller proved he could hand the ball off with the best of them as the Bears rolled to a 10–0 record. Walter Payton rushed for 107 yards and Matt Suhey for 102, the first time in two years that two Bears had broken 100 yards in the same game. The Bears ran 21 consecutive rushing plays before calling a pass, and they wound up running 55 times while throwing just 13. That made perfect sense. The Lions were the worst team in the NFL against the rush. Suhey proved that with six runs of 10 yards or more.

The William Perry extravaganza continued, though with a bit less flash. Late in the first quarter, the Bears had the ball at the Lions' 4-yard line. On came Perry. The Fridge lined up at left halfback and led the blocking, but Payton was stymied at the 2. The Bears needed seven plays, including a holding penalty against Detroit, to reach the end zone. Perry played on three of them, and he went in motion as a decoy on Fuller's one-yard touchdown keeper.

Cold, misty Soldier Field weather gave both teams trouble holding on to the ball, as each side fumbled three times, losing two. Barely into the second quarter, the Lions already had fumbled twice and thrown an interception. Granted, the Lions did not present much competition. But Buddy Ryan's defense held its fifth straight opponent to 10 or fewer points, forced four turnovers, recorded four sacks, and gave up barely 100 total yards.

Matt Suhey, who rushed for 102 yards, rips off a large gain during the Bears' victory over the Lions.

starting tight end Emery Moorehead, who joined McMahon on the sidelines with injuries.

During warmups, McMahon tossed a few left-handed passes but did not test his right shoulder. It would be up to Fuller to lead the Bears for the next two games, in which they would post their most overwhelming victories ... until the Super Bowl. ■

Chicago 24, Detroit 3
NOV. 10, 1985, AT SOLDIER FIELD

BOTTOM LINE
Bears' offense clicks even without McMahon

KEY PLAY Steve Fuller's one-yard TD run
in the first quarter. Playing in place of the injured Jim McMahon, Fuller also scored the Bears' final touchdown.

KEY STAT The Bears outgained the Lions
by an overwhelming 360–106 margin.

Still, Fuller deserves some credit. Not only did his offense outrush Detroit 250–68, he also outpassed Eric Hipple 112–73 and threw no interceptions to his opponent's two. Fuller also scored the first and last touchdowns on bootlegs. He did this without starting flanker Dennis McKinnon or

Mike Ditka said on November 11 that he would take a wait-and-see attitude toward starting quarterback Jim McMahon in Dallas the next week, when the Bears could clinch the NFC Central with a victory against the Cowboys (above). An injured Jim McMahon watches from the sideline (right).

STEVE MCMICHAEL

No. 76, defensive tackle

"This thing isn't going to die out, this '85 Bears thing, baby. We were entertainers, you understand? We were entertainers as well as a great football team. That's why everybody remembers us in the pantheon of pro football. We could've been the team of the decade if McMahon had stayed healthy. But he didn't."

———

"I knew there was going to be something special downtown when we left the airport and all the exits from O'Hare to downtown were blocked off. There was no traffic. There was no traffic even waiting to come on where it was blocked off. So I knew everybody was downtown."

———

"Mike Ditka brought the 'Monsters of the Midway' back to Chicago. They'd been gone since Dick Butkus. That's why he's beloved."

———

"Listen, baby, we were vicious. That's the Cro-Magnon that Hampton talked about, and teams were scared to come in here and play us."

———

"I'm not talking about scared whether they were going to win or lose. I'm talking about scared if they were going to get out of the game walking or on a stretcher."

———

"When Wilber Marshall hit Joe Ferguson in Detroit, ooohhh, my goodness. You can't do it anymore, but it was legal back then. Ferguson was out before he hit the ground, and how I knew he was out was Richard Dent, like a referee in boxing, he picked up Ferguson's arm and let it go and it just flopped back down."

———

"I think we put out six starting quarterbacks that year."

———

"They gave me the paper that we wanted Halas to keep Buddy no matter who the coach was, and I signed it, even though Buddy wasn't playing me yet. That's the kind of respect I had for him. I wanted him to stick around long enough for him to put me in the game and play me. Then I knew I'd done something. I was proud of myself when that happened."

———

"One of the best games I played in pro football was that year against the San Francisco 49ers in

Candlestick Park. I got a game ball and we beat them 26–10. That's when I knew we were going to win the Super Bowl, because they were the defending world champions, they were there in all their glory, they didn't have any injuries, it was in their house, and we whipped their (butts)."

"Buddy would give us a little speech before the game and walk out of the meeting, and Dale Haupt, the defensive line coach, would run the projector and we'd watch one more reel of film. Well, the night before the Super Bowl, Buddy got up in front of us, and the last thing he said before he walked out of the room was, 'No matter what happens, you guys will always be my heroes.' I knew he was gone. Tears in his eyes, you understand?"

"After he walked out and closed the door, I stood up, picked up the metal chair that was under me, those folding chairs, and threw it into the blackboard that was right in front of me. It was like a movie special effect. I was trying to shatter the board. All four legs impaled the thing and just hung there. The room erupted. That's when Hampton clubbed the projector and said, 'This meeting's over.' And we all filed out yelling and screaming. That fever pitch that started right there kind of carried through till about halftime, and we'd already blown the game out."

"I might not ever be in the Hall of Fame, but there's guys in there that are, and I've whipped their (butts)."

"In every Shakespearean tragedy, there's some comic relief, and that's what William Perry was for us."

"'Mongo' I got from the Bears' practices and fighting all the time."

"You know why most wrestlers have long hair and it's flowing? It sells better when you sell the fake punch."

"All-Pro, Super Bowl champion, Monster of the Midway. That's the triple crown, baby." ■

chapter XII

We Can Do Almost Everything, but Maybe We Can't Dance

The Indianapolis Colts didn't stand a chance. They were the Bears' next opponent, at Soldier Field, and they weren't a very good team. And the Bears were seething. The final score was 17–10 Bears, but it wasn't that close. Chicago had been leading 17–3, until the Colts scored on a 61-yard pass late in the fourth quarter. Other than that play, the Colts gained only 24 yards and made one first down in the second half. Walter Payton rushed for his ninth straight 100-yard game, extending his NFL record. And praise be! Jim McMahon played the entire game.

Next up were the New York Jets, a 10–4 team that featured long-haired and flaky defensive end Mark Gastineau, known for sacking quarterbacks and doing a spastic celebratory dance afterward. Ditku had called the Indianapolis win "ugly," and the game against the Jets was no beauty, either. It was close until Kevin Butler made his third and fourth field goals of the game in the last four minutes. The Bears won 19–6. Everything seemed tainted since the Miami loss, but still, the fact was there: the Bears were a 14–1 team.

"By the end of the season if you said 'Refrigerator,' people didn't think of a place to put food. They thought of a huge guy who ate food. That's how famous he was." —Ditka on William Perry

There were so many great players on that 1985 team, and I sometimes wish I could just tell the world how much they meant to me. Take Butthead. Kevin Butler was like one of the guys. You may say, so what? But kickers are often very unusual people. They're guys who are hard to have conversations with. If you're not careful, they'll start crying or calling for their mother. That's if you can even understand what in the hell they're saying, because they're usually from Austria or somewhere. But Butler was born in Savannah, Georgia, and he went out with the guys and partied and was a football player, the real deal. I liked him. Of course, maybe I wouldn't have liked him so much if he couldn't kick straight. But in that Jets game alone he had four field goals. Not real long ones, but needed ones. And he was automatic. Twelve points. Not bad.

William Perry was settling in, doing whatever we asked of him. People might have thought I was all over the map, using this kid like I was. But in the Jets game he picked up a fumble and ran with it seven yards. He may have looked like a barrel rolling across the floor, but he was moving pretty good, in my opinion. I'd already talked to the press about wanting him to run for a touchdown, catch a touchdown pass, and—here was the big one—throw a TD pass. It was fun, but here are two things. One, by doing that it made the other team have to prepare for him and maybe forget about what was really important. And two, I could have done the same thing with 10 other guys, but it wouldn't have worked. It worked with William because he was a good enough athlete and a good enough person to handle it. By the end of the season if you said "Refrigerator," people didn't think of a place to put food. They thought of a huge guy who ate food. That's how famous he was.

You think I was eccentric? You think I was intense? Hell, I remember coming back from a loss up in Minnesota when I was a rookie. Coach Halas got on the intercom at the front of the airplane and said, "You're nothing but a bunch of c---s!" I think Michael McCaskey, his own grandson and president of the team, once said I was a lot calmer than Halas.

I suppose I was a product of where I grew up and how I grew up. My dad was old school, absolutely. He was a former Marine. He never went to battle, but he was a Marine. He worked on a railroad that serviced J & L Steel in Aliquippa, which is one of the mill towns up the Ohio River from Pittsburgh. My dad was a car repair man, a welder. A burner is what we called them. His dad was a burner, too, did the same thing.

Dad would come home, and his clothes always had holes in them from the sparks. He had burn marks on his hands and arms, but that's what he did. He was self-taught. I think he went to the seventh grade, at most. But he could do any crossword puzzle I've ever seen. He had a great vocabulary, and with that limited education he became president of his union. Although he defended the workers, he wouldn't defend somebody who wouldn't work. You slept on the job? I got news for you. Pop Ditka was on your ass.

We are Ukranian. My father was born here, but his parents came over from the old country. People called us Polacks, mostly, or Hunkies. I don't know why they couldn't come up with Ukies. We weren't a close family, and it was because my dad was tough. He was tough with my mom. And he was tough with me. He got on me hard, but he

didn't go after the other kids. I was the oldest, and I had two brothers and a sister. I was talking to my sister the other day, and I said, "Dad never touched you, did he?"

And she said, "One time when I was a sophomore or junior in high school I said something to him, and he slapped me."

I said, "I never thought he slapped anyone but me."

I know he never touched the other two boys. But he was rough with me and my mom. When you see that as a kid, it bothers you. But then in retrospect you understand that he was raised like that, and that's what he knew. I blamed him for a lot. I didn't like him, basically, until I went off to college and lived away from home. All of my buddies got to do stuff, but I could never be out past nine o'clock until high school. There was a reason why he did it, but I didn't understand his motives until the end: he didn't want me working in the mill. He wanted me to get an education. We kids were going to have a better life than he did.

It took a long time for that to sink in, to explain things to myself, but the more I understood, the better it got. At the end we used to talk a lot, and we had a great relationship even though it was from a distance. It's like that song, "Cat's in the Cradle," by Harry Chapin. When I had time for him, he had no time for me. When he had time for me, I had no time for him. That's the sadness of getting old with your kids. You can't go back and undo things. But, really, we went from being strangers to being friends by the end.

He died 11 years ago, at 80, while I was coaching in New Orleans. He had hardening of the arteries, and he was a four-packs-of-Lucky-Strikes-a-day guy from the time he was 12 until he quit cold turkey at age 59. Twenty-one years without a

One time me and my buddies went to the library during the holidays just to mess around. They had a Christmas tree up, and we stole a couple of ornaments. Why, I don't know. We were dumb-ass kids. So we have these little glass ornaments, those colored balls, and we're running down the street playing catch with them, throwing them back and forth. You know how light they are, and the wind is blowing. So I throw one, and the wind catches it, and it hits a kid right above his

"When I went nuts on teammates or players, it was only because winning was so important to me." —Ditka

smoke, which was pretty good. And he used to go crazy when Diana would light up a cigarette in front of him. He'd shake his head and say, "I'd give anything to have one of those!"

I was the firstborn, and probably he was hardest on me for two reasons: because I was the oldest and because I deserved it more than the other ones. I had a knack for getting into stupid trouble. Nothing malicious. But if there was something stupid to do, I'd be one of the guys doing it, and I'd always end up getting blamed. I'll give you an example.

eye. I hit him pretty good. The glass shatters, and he's cut, and there's blood pouring down his face, and he freaks out. He has to get about six stitches.

Me, I have to go to school and tell the nun what happened, and she beats the crap out of me with a ruler. Then I have to go home and tell Dad, and he beats the crap out of me. That's the way it was. I got my butt beat a lot. Now the nuns, maybe they were mean. But I think it was their job to teach you discipline and order, and they didn't allow any messing around. The ones I had, anyway.

Did beating me make me change as a person? No. But it taught me to fear doing something wrong. If you're afraid to do something wrong, you'll avoid it because you don't want your ass whupped. Funny thing is, as a coach I don't believe in it. I know the nuns did, and my dad did, but I don't. I believe that if you're fair with people, you're up front with them, you talk to them, it's better than force. Still, the only way they deterred me from doing even stupider things as a kid was by punishment.

When I went nuts on teammates or players, it was only because winning was so important to me. I got on some guys pretty bad at Pitt, for instance, and I'm not proud of that. But I really couldn't think of another way. I couldn't do it Landry's way. Of course, I didn't know Landry back then. Even Lombardi couldn't have been like Landry. Lombardi was Lombardi. I was myself.

The world can judge you how it wants. I remember we went to London in the summer of 1986. We were playing an exhibition game against the Cowboys at Wembley Stadium for all these ga-ga Englishmen, and we are the rage of the island. This was the NFL's big push into Europe, going global. People had T-shirts with the Fridge on them, No. 72, running with the football. They'd sprint right past Walter Payton to get to Perry.

Everybody was famous, though. Willie Gault had stuff going on, and Matt Suhey visited the stock exchange, and, yes, Walter was very important. But he wasn't literally huge, like Perry. The cover of *Sports Illustrated* even showed Fridge with the Cowboys' "Too Tall" Jones standing next to one of the Queen's Royal Guardsmen. I said in a press conference, "I have the best running back in the history of the game, and all you want to know about is a lineman!"

So anyway, back to 1985. Around the time of our Jets game, Gastineau was getting all of the pub. That didn't bother me. He was a good player, but the New York media made him a lot better than he was. I mean, he couldn't carry Dent's or Hampton's jock strap. He's got a sack dance? Why would you want to do that if you're good and you know it? What does waving your arms around have to do with anything? *Look at me, I'm great!* Prove it by playing.

People said I was doing too many off-field things? My team was? If you still play hard on Sunday, which is when the games are played, that's all that matters. If the players can make a few bucks off the field, good. As for me, I was fully dedicated. To the critics, I said screw you. Besides, I wasn't doing that much, mostly just the TV show with Johnny.

We had one more regular-season game to go,

against the Lions, who were an average team. It was there in Detroit, in their stupid dome, but if we played our game and never made mistakes like in the Miami game, we couldn't be beat. Before that game the Pro Bowl teams were announced, and we had eight guys make the roster—Payton, Hampton, Dent, Covert, Hilgenberg, Singletary, Wilson, and even Dave Duerson, who was shocked as shit. They all deserved it. But so did Fencik and Van Horne and Marshall and about five other guys.

Some of the hoopla came from another thing, though. A bunch of the guys, 10 of them, including Payton, Fridge, Fuller, and McMahon, had used one of their off-days to make some kind of rap video. It was Willie Gault's idea, I think, along with some producer. Willie had asked me to be in it, but I'd taken a pass. Dancing? Singing? Are you kidding? You can laugh, because I've done a lot of nutty stuff, such as wear a tuxedo in a "wedding portrait" with my "bride," Ricky Williams, and act in a soccer movie. But I didn't give a crap about this thing. Plus, I remembered what that nun had said to me about singing. I didn't even know what this video was about, but real soon I see these giant ads and it's called "The Super Bowl Shuffle"!

My God, we have another regular-season game to play and then we'll have to win two more games in the playoffs just to go to the Super Bowl. Talk about jumping the gun. But hey, I admired the guys' confidence, if that's what it was. A lot of people already hated us. Like I

seemed to be saying more and more: *screw 'em.*

So we go to Detroit and we win our finale 37–17. Dennis Gentry—little Pinkie—runs a kickoff back for a touchdown, the first against the Lions in five years. And Wilbur Marshall hits quarterback Joe Ferguson so hard right under the chin that you can see Ferguson is unconscious even before he hits the turf. When Wilbur got fined later by the league, I thought it was bullcrap. I mean, the refs hadn't even called a penalty.

It was an odd game. Even though we won pretty easily, the game bothered me. It was blah. I was certain a good team would beat us, maybe embarrass us. Well, I wasn't certain of that, but I feared it. I couldn't get the Dolphins game out of my mind. William Perry even picked up a fumble and ran until somebody jumped on him. But it didn't matter.

The locker room was very quiet. Everybody knew we had only one goal now that we no longer could go undefeated. And this little win had nothing to do with it. "Maybe we shouldn't do too many 'Super Bowl Shuffles,'" I said to the media. I didn't mean that. But I didn't want this thing to get away from us. I was tense and cranky.

We would have home-field advantage all through the playoffs, and we were going to start off against the winner of the 49ers-Giants wild-card game. We had two weeks to kill.

We needed to get shuffling. ■

Chicago 44, Dallas 0
Bears Destroy Dallas

Mike Ditka played for Dallas for four years and coached there under Tom Landry for nine more. But perhaps no game had more meaning for him than the Bears' lopsided victory in Game 11. In Ditka's first regular-season visit to Texas Stadium since his coaching stint ended, his Bears handed the Cowboys their worst defeat in franchise history and their first shutout in 15 years.

How dominant was the Bears' defense? Midway through the fourth quarter of a 44-point uprising, the Bears had scored only one offensive touchdown. Richard Dent and Mike Richardson returned first-half interceptions for touchdowns, and punter Maury Buford continually pinned the Cowboys in uncomfortable positions.

The result: Dallas never penetrated beyond the Bears' 38-yard line. In fact, five of the Cowboys' first six running plays failed to achieve the line of scrimmage.

Early in the second quarter, linebacker Otis Wilson collared Danny White on a blitz. The quarterback was knocked out when he hit the turf. White returned to start the second half, but Wilson knocked him out again. While White sat, the Bears tormented backup Gary Hogeboom into three interceptions.

Meanwhile, the offense put 378 total yards on the board and controlled the ball for 35:18, all with Jim McMahon sitting out again with a sore shoulder. Steve Fuller threw for 164 yards and kept a steady hand on the offensive throttle.

Otis Wilson swivels the head of the Cowboys' Danny White during a third-quarter sack, knocking White from the game.

Kevin Butler kicked three field goals. His first was a career-long 44 yards. Then he bested that with a 46-yarder. Walter Payton gained 100 yards for the sixth game in a row, one short of the NFL record. He finished with 132 rushing yards on 22 carries.

The Bears' 11–0 start was the NFL's best since 1972 and allowed them to clinch the NFC Central with five weeks remaining. But Ditka's best memory had to be the sight of fair-weather Dallas fans streaming toward the exits after three quarters, their team hopelessly behind. ■

Chicago 44, Dallas 0
NOV. 17, 1985, AT TEXAS STADIUM

BOTTOM LINE
Coach's roots make blowout win special

KEY PLAY
Dan Hampton's force of a Danny White interception. The defensive end cartwheeled his blocker, jumped into White's face, and batted the ball, which Richard Dent grabbed for the one-yard touchdown that started the rout.

KEY STAT
The Bears intercepted three passes in the first half.

Late in the first half, Ditka sent William Perry into the offensive lineup. On first down from the 2, Perry took a handoff to the 1-yard line. Fuller plunged in on the next play, and it was 24–0 with nearly three minutes left until halftime. The rout was so complete that Ditka rested Fuller for the last 10 minutes in favor of rookie Mike Tomczak.

Willie Gault catches a pass in front of Cowboys defender Ron Fellows (above). Even an assist from William Perry can't quite lift Walter Payton into the end zone (right).

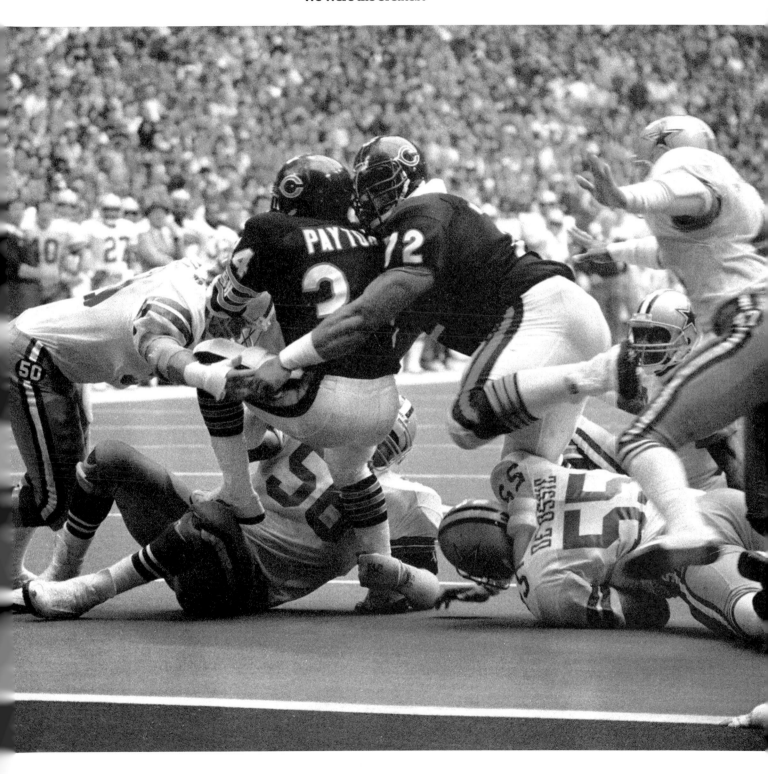

KEITH VAN HORNE

No. 78, offensive tackle

"That year was the highlight of my football career and the low point of my personal life. My dad passed away on the 28th of December. The fact that we still had to play was probably a good thing for me because I could just focus on that, because I was in another world. The last years of his life, we kind of got close and took it to a different level."

———————

"That generation, I think you know what I'm talking about, kept things in. But it got to the point when I went to college that that started changing. I was on my own. I had some independence, could say yes or no to any advice he might give me. But you start realizing how smart your parents are because you start experiencing things they talked to you about when you thought they don't know what they're talking about, and then you find out, well, I guess they actually did. Once the game was over, I went right to the locker room and started grieving. It was a huge relief to get it over with.

I miss him still. He was a good man."

———————

"Here's the second part: Andy Frederick, who was our backup at tackle, got hurt in pregame warmups, so Jimbo Covert and I looked at each other and said, 'Oh, God. We don't have anyone to replace us.' I had to play the whole game."

———————

"Shame on us. I think Dan Hampton said that— shame on us for not going back—and he's right."

———————

"Our defense developed into probably the best defense that ever played. Certainly in the top two or three ever. It was fun watching them. You could see the fear in the eyes of opposing offenses, the quarterbacks especially."

———————

"People talk about our defense all the time, and rightfully so. But we led the league in time of possession, led the league in scoring, led the league in rushing. So we were able to do some stuff, too."

"Part of the reason we were able to run the ball so well is we had to practice against those guys. And our practices were not like I think they practice today. We had Ditka, so we were out there hitting each other."

—————

"Jim McMahon knew football. He could come out and audible or change the play that was sent in if he didn't like it, which didn't always go over so well with Ditka. But I think Jim had a better grasp of it than [offensive coordinator] Ed Hughes and Mike Ditka, let me tell you."

—————

"Up in Green Bay when [William Perry] went in, he ran right over me and just nailed me in the back. I scored as well."

—————

"Walter was the real deal. He was the workhorse. I've been very blessed, very honored. I blocked for Charlie White and Marcus Allen in college. They both won a Heisman Trophy. Then I got to come to Chicago and got to block for the greatest all-around running back that ever played, in my opinion."

—————

"I'm proud and honored to be a part of Chicago history." ■

chapter XIII

Headband Craziness, a Yuppie Who Likes to Hurt People, the Elephant in the Snow

As the New York Giants wild-card game against the defending Super Bowl champion San Francisco 49ers was ending, fans at the Meadowlands in East Rutherford, New Jersey, began chanting, "We want the Bears! We want the Bears!" The Giants had been impressive in smacking the 49ers 17–3. But the fact that so many of the 76,000 howling fans actually wanted a piece of the 15–1 Bears showed a certain audacity that could only come from the safety of a bleacher seat and a throat warmed by a flask of booze.

The Bears had gone to the Atlanta Falcons training camp in Suwanee, Georgia, to practice for the first round.

Ditka had wanted to set up camp at the University of Illinois in Champaign, but the plastic bubble that was needed to cover the field couldn't be erected in time. No matter. It was just geography. The Bears hadn't changed from what they were. They may have lost to the Dolphins and had internal squabbling that was embarrassing and unprofessional, but they hadn't died. They had been nicked, frustrated, lowered half a notch, and they were angry.

Mike Singletary had been chosen NFL Defensive Player of the Year. Ditka was soon to be named NFL Coach of the Year. The Bears were being given early credit for the machine they had become, yet they had an edge that was sharp and unyielding. And Jim McMahon—of course—was as surly as ever. He greeted the press at the Bears' new site by telling assembled members they basically disgusted him and asking where they were spending New Year's Eve, so he could avoid that spot. He then added that all of them were "worried about what everybody thinks. I can give a shit about what everybody thinks."

On a cheerier note, Richard Meyer, president of Red Label Records, which had produced the 23-minute "Super Bowl Shuffle" video shot at the Park West Theater in Chicago, announced that the tape had already shipped "triple platinum," and that 550,000 separate audio cassettes had been distributed. Another million of the things—

Gary Fencik Remembers '85
The Playoff Game Against the Giants

"It was a really cold and windy day with bright sun. We knew points were going to be hard to come by, and the Giants had a very good team with Phil Simms, running back Joe Morris, Lawrence Taylor.

"All week Buddy gave us a great game plan. He said, 'To stop the Giants we have to tackle really well. We have to stop number 20.' That was Morris. 'That guy has 21 touchdowns, compared to Walter Payton who has nine but is only the best player in the history of the NFL? We take number 20 away and we'll whip their asses! They may have the No. 2 defense in the league, but we're No. 1. Take no prisoners!'

"We were fired up, but the play of the special teams turned it around. Because we knew it would be so hard to score, when Shaun recovered that blown punt for a touchdown, it just seemed like a huge advantage. You can shank a punt or get one blocked or nearly miss one. But to whiff like that? Amazing."

videos and tapes—were soon to come. The rap, with the Bears performers in full uniforms, but without helmets and shoulder pads, had shocked everyone by becoming a national hit. Apparently lyrics such as Otis Wilson's "The girls all love me, for my body and my mind," had captivated sports fans throughout the land. Or perhaps it was the refrain—"We're not here to cause no trouble, we're just doin' the Super Bowl Shuffle!"—replete with Fridge's gap-toothed smile and Steve Fuller's pitiful boogeying—that got people excited.

In truth, Fuller had a reason for his ineptitude. The players had filmed the dance the day after the Miami loss (talk about chutzpa), and he was still injured. Aficionados of this kind of thing can study the video closely and notice the bandage still on the hobbling Fuller's foot and ankle. McMahon—"I'm the punky QB"—and Payton had been mixed into the group electronically, since they had done their versions later than the other players. Payton's was done the next day at the Park West, but McMahon's was shot using a blue screen inside a Halas Hall racquetball court. The proceeds of the venture were to be split with the players and various charities—but the accounting, the artists would find out, would be a mess for years.

Not so with game preparation. "Tempers have flared," said Ditka with satisfaction. "Guys are on edge." That was what he wanted, what he felt was needed to complete this journey.

We practiced anywhere during that season. It didn't matter. We had the one grass field behind the offices there in Lake Forest, but the college team would play its games there on Saturdays, and sometimes the field was torn to crap. When it rained or there was lightning, sometimes we'd go into the college gym and run our stuff in sneakers.

But as it got later in the season and the field got more torn up and then frozen solid and we couldn't really accomplish much in a gym, we would go down to South Park, which was about half a mile or so from Halas Hall. It wasn't the location for that cartoon or whatever the hell it is on TV. It was just a neighborhood park. It had tennis courts and jungle gyms and moms walking their babies and dogs sniffing around and all that stuff. But it had a lot of grass, and we could at least run our plays. To get there you had to wind around through the neighborhood and make sure you didn't make a wrong turn and end up in Lake Michigan or Iowa. Guys would commandeer golf carts to get there, or a bunch would jump in the back of the equipment truck and ride along with their legs hanging out. Most everybody else swiped a bike from somewhere or just walked. I guess we should have used the sidewalks, but it was a sleepy suburban neighborhood, so the mighty Chicago Bears would come straggling down the middle of these neighborhood roads, carrying helmets, laughing and goofing around, headed to work.

Kids would come around, and mailmen would honk to get through. It was a sight. Of course, if the McCaskeys had spent a little more money on a bigger place, we wouldn't have had to make our

"We're not here to cause no trouble, we're just doin' the Super Bowl Shuffle!"

trek. But the Halas Hall facility had been a decent improvement over other NFL sites when it was built in the 1970s, so you couldn't really complain. We played our games at Soldier Field on artificial turf, though, and what we got eventually for practice purposes was a patch of turf about 10 feet by 10 feet on the sideline of our grass field. That really helped. Whoo boy.

But if you're on a mission, what difference does any of it make? It's in your hearts and your heads.

Now it was January, though, and everything in Chicago was frozen like cement. South Park might as well have been a skating rink.

So we went down to Suwanee and practiced before the Giants game, just to keep from freezing to death. That was fine. Most of the work was done, you see. A team defines itself as a season goes on. You have preseason to get in shape and find the right players, and then you get the offense and defense you want, and then you work to make it come together during the regular season. But you don't suddenly become something you're not. The leopard ain't changing its spots. So you tweak and fine-tune.

Buddy and I were okay again. But the tension, I suppose, would never go away entirely. He was a very stubborn, proud man. And so am I. And he wanted to be a head coach. And why not? So be it. The ending could be what all of us wanted.

One guy who was making some noise was Dennis McKinnon. He wasn't real happy about how little he was being used lately. I loved Dennis, and maybe it's because he was a feisty s.o.b. He didn't weigh much, he was like a slender point guard in basketball, but he would block your ass off downfield or anywhere. Just ask Lawrence Taylor. And he had very soft hands and a knack for getting open and making big plays.

The thing was he'd had arthroscopic knee surgery in early July, and the fact he was back and playing at all was amazing. Football's a tough game, and feelings get hurt. Dennis had seven touchdown catches in the first seven weeks of the season, but in the last seven games he had only seven catches, period, and no TDs. Did that mean he hadn't been a huge part of our team, or wasn't still a huge part? No. But he had to shut up and play, like everybody else. Teamwork. Teamwork. Look, just a few days after my DUI arrest, I had my 46th birthday, and guess what somebody gave me? A "Get Out of Jail Free" card. So I laughed about it.

It was funny. Embarrassing, but funny. Come on, Dennis. Only three more weeks.

Another guy who had been a tremendous blessing to our team was tight end Tim Wright-man. Everybody always said the Bears couldn't find a tight end ever since old No. 89 moved on, but Tim did a great job for us. He had a big touch-down catch for us in the Jets game, and he had a streak of at least one catch in eight games, the longest for any receiver on our team. He and Emery Moorehead split a lot of time at tight end, and God knows I loved Emery to death. The stuff he gave us was so much more than a coach would ever count on, and when you get it—you just smile.

Emery was the starter in 14 of our 16 games, and he had been a nobody, just a sixth-round pick by the Giants back in 1977. We got him for noth-ing, and all he did for us was everything we asked. See, everybody knows about the stars. They glorify the big names. That's all the stupid media does. But players like Moorehead and Wrightman and McKinnon are the foundation of any team. What are you going to do without them? Lose.

We go back to Chicago for the game, and the city is really cranked up. The lions in front of the Art Institute have Bears helmets on, and all you hear every second of the day is that "Super Bowl Shuffle" thing going on and on. Me, I would rather hear some Sinatra or Nat King Cole, but what the hell. The Fridge rapping, "I'm no dumb cookie," is entertaining, I suppose.

At Soldier Field it's cold and windy, like you'd expect on a January day. People who don't know about the Midwest and the Great Lakes may not have a clue about wind coming in off Lake Michigan or the wind swirling around in places like Cleveland or Buffalo off Lake Erie. In Chicago, Soldier Field is right next to the lake, and the cold wind will come in and do whatever it wants. Sometimes you'll see flags blowing in all four directions. So kickers and quarterbacks better be prepared for it.

Early in the game we back the Giants up toward their own goal at the north end, and it's fourth down. The wind is gusting, and it's some-thing like 14 below zero windchill, but, hell, this is Chicago in the winter, in the playoffs. Get your skirts off. Focus. Forget the damn cold. The snap comes back for Sean Landetta, their punter, and we've got a punt block rush on from the left side with Shaun Gayle and Dennis Gentry. They pick up the rushers, but Landetta is worried or hurried or something, and he goes to punt the ball, and he swings his leg as hard as he can and misses it. He misses the freaking ball. Maybe he gets a tiny piece of it, but the wind just moves the ball to the side, and it looked like Charlie Brown trying to kick the ball after Lucy yanks it away.

Gayle picks up the thing at the 5 and runs it in for a touchdown. We're ahead 7–0, and on this day that's all we're going to need. Our defense is back in its full attack mode. The Giants will rush for a total of 32 yards. And Richard Dent himself will have three and a half sacks for minus-38 yards. Do the math on that one. McMahon is wearing gloves, which is something I'm not sure I've seen a lot of quarterbacks do, but he throws two touchdown passes to McKinnon. See, I told Dennis to hang in there. The funny thing is, Mac is throwing better spirals than ever. Usually he threw a ball that wobbled around like a ruptured duck, but these were almost the way a pro quarterback was supposed to throw.

Yeah, there's wind like in a tornado in the stadium, and Kevin Butler misses every one of his field-goal attempts. So I understand how Landetta could screw up like that. But other guys have to step up in these kind of conditions. I told Butthead after the game not to kill himself, to throw the gun away if he had one. It's just a golf shot, I said. It'll come back.

Of course, I was feeling pretty good because we had whipped the Giants and their outstanding coach, Bill Parcells, 21–0. Talk about defense. The Giants never converted a third down the entire game. Oh for 12. How could they possibly win? I do recall that Fridge was playing on defense and hit their little running back Joe Morris like a runaway cement truck. Kind of sad when that happens. Otis Wilson had a funny line about it. He

said he looked down at Morris, "and I thought it was a poster of him."

Now we were 16–1 and ready for our next step. That would be against the Los Angeles Rams the next Sunday. I was feeling okay, but then the nerves took over again. Where were we now? We were the owners of an amazing record. We were division champs. We had the best defense in the league, the best running back, the best of a lot of things. But we were right back where we were the year before. It was the NFC Championship Game coming up, against another West Coast team. I couldn't live through another game like the San Francisco game from last season. And I knew guys like Payton and Singletary couldn't, either.

Or a guy like free safety Gary Fencik. He was a Yale guy who had his MBA from Northwestern, and you would probably think he was some yuppie pinhead sissy who didn't give a damn and just wanted to look pretty. But he was another ferocious guy. Hell, coming into 1985 he already had more tackles than any Bear ever, even Dick Butkus. He and Doug Plank used to run into receivers just for fun. Just to see if they could knock them out.

Fencik was writing a column for one of the newspapers, which was appropriate because he was the brains of our defense. In that NFC game out in San Francisco in 1984 Gary had four tackles, an assist, two passes broken up, and two interceptions. If we'd won, he probably would have been MVP. If we'd won. Fencik didn't want to go out like Ernie Banks, like Gayle Sayers, like Jerry Sloan, like Ron Santo, or any of those other Chicago stars who had never won the championship game.

We were everybody's biggest target, including, I'm sure, the Rams. And remember, they were out in Los Angeles then, not St. Louis. A lot of people loved us, but I think a lot of people hated us, too. Maybe I'm wrong about that. I was really a guy with blinders on at that time, not caring about the rest of the world. Just our own little world.

The genius oddsmakers had made us 10-point favorites over L.A., but they didn't have to play. The Rams had Eric Dickerson at tailback, and he was one of the best runners in the history of the NFL. In their last game he'd run for 248 yards. I respected their coach, John Robinson, too. He'd come to the NFL after coaching at Southern Cal and taking them to three Rose Bowl championships in seven years. But deep down inside I felt this year was different. Yeah, we were playing another huge game to see if we could get into the Super Bowl. But this time we were playing it at home. We were the top dogs in this one. That's right, all of those regular-season wins weren't just for show. They meant something.

Then, too, L.A. was starting a guy named

Dieter Brock at quarterback, a 34-year-old rookie, who had come into the NFL from the Canadian League. I'm sorry, but with our defense, that was like throwing a pork chop into a dog pound. I may have told our team that. I'm sure Buddy did. But we didn't say anything publicly.

I started talking about us being the Grabowskis. I meant it. We were the common man. And now the common man was going to do something the fancy man could only hope to do.

The game started, and it was a cold, gray day, and I remember it looked like it could snow at any second.

McMahon had been fined by the NFL front office $5,000 for wearing a headband that said "Adidas" on in it during a previous game. I don't know why he wore it. Probably to make money. So in this game he's got the Adidas thing around his neck, and when he takes his helmet off I see he's got a new stretchy thing around his forehead. This one says, "ROZELLE." There's no explaining this guy. I mean, Pete Rozelle is the freaking commissioner of the league. And he's at the game, watching.

But I suppose it was sort of fun, and I heard later Rozelle loved it. It was pretty clever, I uppose, and about the most interesting thing McMahon could do after being ordered not to wear signs on his head.

You need discipline on a team, but as I've said

"I see he's got a new stretchy thing around his forehead. This one says, 'ROZELLE.' There's no explaining this guy. I mean, Pete Rozelle is the freaking commissioner of the league. And he's at the game, watching." —Ditka on McMahon

all along, McMahon was a different duck. He was the most devious person in the world, and he'd always find a way to get under your skin. Mine, Rozelle's, the opponents', everybody's. To be honest, though, I think Walter sometimes wore a headband that said "Kangaroo" on it, a shoe company that gave him a car when he broke Jim Brown's all-time rushing record. They paid him a lot of money, so why shouldn't he advertise their company? I just don't like the way the league lets guys make idiots of themselves in all of these end zone things, all of these dumb celebrations, and then uses it to promote the NFL. Why should they care what your helmet or T-shirt says? You know why? They're not getting their cut of the money. That's why it bothers them. You want to straighten things out, then cut out everything—all of the promotion. Just make it football. Is that asking too much?

I remember when the NFL wouldn't let the 49ers' former coach, Mike Nolan, wear a suit on the sideline. They said they'd fine him, because he had to wear official NFL issue. That's just flat-out embarrassing to the NFL. Mike Nolan's dad, Dick, was a great coach in the league, and he wore a suit, and his son was trying to honor him. It's disrespectful to Tom Landry, to Vince Lombardi, to Buddy Parker, hell, to George Halas. They all wore suits on the sideline. The NFL is all about marketing now, not being reasonable.

One reason I was such a Mike Nolan fan is he hired one of my favorite players for his staff, one of my favorite people in life, current 49ers coach Mike Singletary. Another one of my favorites, Les Frazier, got his first shot at coaching in the NFL under Tony Dungy in Indianapolis. Les was one of the most underrated cornerbacks ever. He had six interceptions in that 1985 season, and he would get another one off Brock against the Rams. Nice guy, and I'm thrilled he's back in the game (as the Vikings' defensive coordinator). And Singletary—you know how I feel, and I'll tell you more about him in a minute.

But thinking about individualism always

Gary Fencik Remembers '85

NFC Championship Win Over the Rams

"That NFC Championship Game against the Rams was amazing. We had stopped Dickerson and that offense and we had this feeling of near invincibility. Two games into the playoffs and we hadn't allowed a point? That's pretty good.

"But then on that fumble at the end, where Richard knocked the ball loose and Wilber spun around and picked it up, and here I am running along with everybody else, and the snow's coming down and the crowd is roaring, and it seemed to take so long, like take forever, and I'm running and I'm thinking, *We're going to the Super Bowl.* We knew Wilber was going to score and he's running and everybody's running and it was just amazing, the way it all came together.

"When I think back on myself in those days, I am always reminded that I was in a system that allowed me to excel. I don't know how many people are aware of this but back in 1983 when we knew our head coach Neil Armstrong was going to be let go and there were going to be some major changes take place, Allen Page and I wrote a letter to George Halas and everybody on the defense signed it, and we just asked that whatever happened we would appreciate it very much if Mr. Halas would see fit to keep Buddy Ryan as our defensive coach. He

did, and then later he hired Ditka as the head coach. But keeping Buddy was very important to our success.

"Buddy made everything contingent on keeping the other team's offense off-balance, fearful, never knowing what was coming next. We blitzed from everywhere and we gave quarterbacks only a second or two to make decisions. It got to the point that quarterbacks were almost helpless. Teams were still using straight drop backs and there just wasn't enough time for quarterbacks to run their normal offenses.

"At free safety, my position, you're back twelve yards and you're able to observe this thing happening in front of you. In some ways you're the only player who can see everything, see it all. And then you realize—pre-snap—because of the call and the way it's setting up in front of you: *Oh my God they're not gonna be able to cover this blitz.* Before anything has happened you can see this. It's over. They've got one back in and he can't block everybody and he has to make a choice, and he doesn't even know where they're coming from yet! I'm watching the quarterback and wondering where he's going. Then I realize he's going down!

"By the end we were almost unstoppable. And I could see it all."

brings me back to McMahon. He had a great ability to recognize defenses, and when he saw something he knew was wrong or weak, he knew how to exploit it. But the main thing is he was not at all reluctant to audible after he saw something. Didn't care at all. Avellini and Harbaugh would put me over the edge with a couple of terrible audibles, but McMahon did it all of the time. And I gave him the freedom to do it. Sometimes I didn't

for a 16-yard touchdown. Hell, the great Eric Dickerson's longest run of the day was nine yards. And no TDs, either.

Then with the score 10–0 in the third quarter, we have the ball again, and it is second and 10 at the Rams' 22. I call a draw play. Give it to Wally, see what he could do. Seems like a no-brainer. But there's McMahon at the line looking around, barking off stuff. Oh Jesus, I know something's

"He got a couple of nice blocks downfield, and this beat-up guy with a knee brace and everything weaved around and dove into the end zone for a 16-yard touchdown." —Ditka on McMahon

understand why I did. But I did. And as a result of that he made some incredible plays for us that year. I guess that's what a creative madman can do if given a chance.

That's what he did early in the first quarter against the Rams. We were down in the red zone, and it was third and 8, and we had a pass play called. McMahon scrambled to his left and faked, looked for receivers, faked, and then he took off running. He got a couple of nice blocks downfield, and this beat-up guy with a knee brace and everything weaved around and dove into the end zone

happening. He's calling an audible. There's the snap, and McMahon moves to his left. Willie Gault is lined up on the left and he runs downfield and gives an inside fake to cornerback LeRoy Irvin, a beautiful post-flag move, and Irvin bites on it, and Jim throws a perfect touchdown pass to Willie in the corner of the end zone. Jim's feet were off the ground when he threw and he was all cockeyed, and his arm went straight across his body, exactly how nobody should ever do it.

I'm a genius, aren't I?

McMahon was pumped up. I remember what

Payton said afterward. "He was a crazy nut out there. He did everything but take his clothes off, and if we'd been out there longer, he might have done that."

Seventeen points was way more than we needed, because the defense had locked down the Rams offense and thrown away the key. Dickerson got a total of 46 yards rushing, and Brock threw for a total of 44 net yards. It was a joke! They had 130 total yards of offense, and our defense even outscored them.

The defensive touchdown came with under three minutes left, and the crowd really started to get excited, realizing we might truly make it this year. Singletary had been playing his usual great game, and I could see that warrior look of determination in his eyes. They didn't call him "Samurai" for nothing. This was a guy who was so intense and focused on being a great football player that at Baylor he broke 16 of his own helmets. During the Rams game he saw some screws lying on the field and didn't realize they came from his own head gear, and his facemask was ready to drop off. He broke his chinstrap after that. And at the end his helmet was cracked. He didn't care.

At one practice in 1984 he was leading the team in calisthenics and he just started screaming, "I refuse to go home early! *I refuse to go home early!*" Can you understand how much this guy wanted it? All of it?

Well, he wasn't going home early this year. Dieter Brock dropped back to pass, and Buddy's dogs came roaring in on him, just like they had all afternoon. Dent smacked the ball away, and Brock went flying. William Perry came lumbering by and tried to pick up the loose ball. It kept bouncing, and finally Wilbur Marshall got it. He shrugged off Dickerson, who was diving for him, and then he took off upfield. Fridge was running with him like a big old elephant, and some other Bears were all around, looking back, like a posse. Singletary must have been somewhere in there, I know he was, and my God, it was beautiful. It had just started snowing, these big, slow flakes coming down like in one of those Christmas snow globes, and it was perfect. Bears weather, Bears dominance, Bears success, Bears kicking ass. If we could have frozen that scene and made it a billboard, it would have captured the season.

We won 24–0. In our two playoff games we had scored 45 points and hadn't given up one.

There were cigars in the locker room, brought by Covert. But it was still subdued. No champagne, no screaming. Lots of hugs, handshakes. Big smiles. But we had one more rung to climb, one more peak. Everybody knew that.

Of course, McMahon said what was on his mind.

"Fuck the champagne, I want a beer." ■

Chicago 36, Atlanta 0
Numbers Add Up to an Even Dozen

After the Bears stomped Atlanta 36–0 at Soldier Field to complete a three-game stretch in which they'd outscored opponents by a combined 104–3, other numbers might pale. No way.

Walter Payton gained 102 yards for his seventh straight game with 100 or more yards, tying the NFL record held by Buffalo's O.J. Simpson and Houston's Earl Campbell. Payton, who left for the day in the third quarter, had his 71st career 100-yard game and scored the Bears' first touchdown by tiptoeing down the sideline for 40 yards, the team's longest run of the season.

The defense suffocated the Falcons, holding them to 119 total yards and neutering the passing game. Atlanta's David Archer and Bob Holly combined to complete three passes for 16 yards, and their passing yardage was reduced to minus-22 when 38 yards of sacks were factored in.

Three of those sacks came from Henry Waechter, who recorded the Bears' third safety in six games.

Henry Waechter! Who knew?

The closest the Falcons penetrated was to the Bears' 18-yard line in the third quarter, but Gerald Riggs, the NFL's leading rusher, was held to one yard on a fourth-and-3 situation.

William Perry added a wrinkle to his offensive legend by scoring again, this time by leaping (everything's relative) into the end zone from the 1-yard line. Having been ankle-tackled and stopped short of the goal the previous week in

Defensive lineman Mike Hartenstine grabs a fumble by Atlanta's Bob Holly.

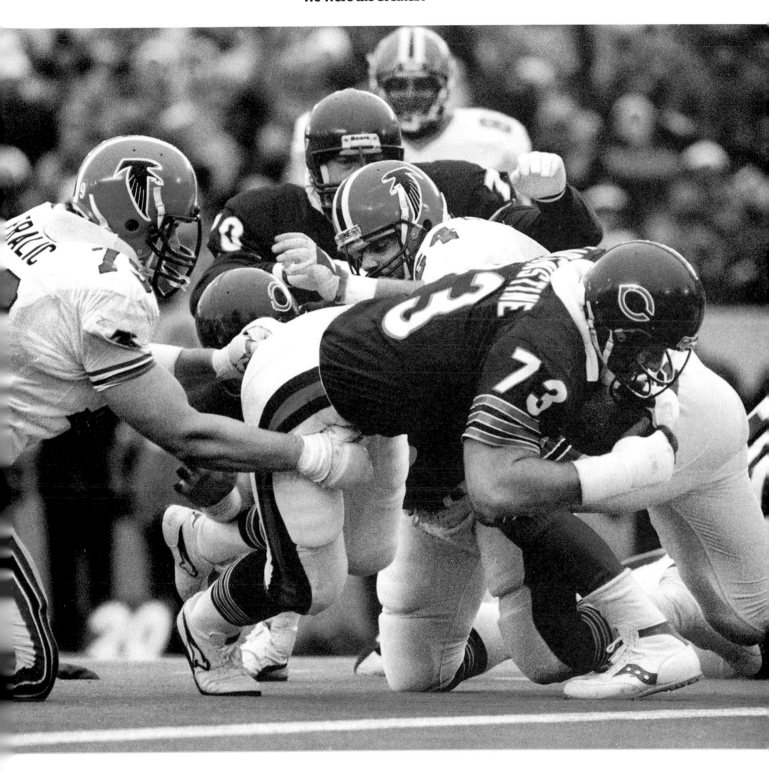

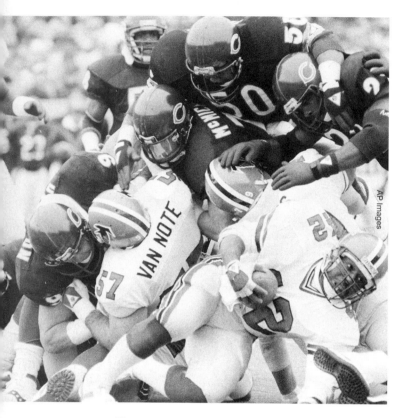

run helped set up the first of two Kevin Butler field goals, and Thomas himself scored on a two-yard run in the second half.

The rout of the Falcons was the 12th consecutive victory for the Bears. Only two teams in NFL history had won more at the start of a season, the Bears' 13 in 1934 and the Miami Dolphins' 14 in 1972.

"Right now we're playing at a very high peak," defensive end Dan Hampton said. "We needed this type of effort to get ready for Miami because they're a great offensive team."

Eight days later, Hampton's words would prove prophetic. ■

Chicago 36, Atlanta 0
NOV. 24, 1985, AT SOLDIER FIELD

BOTTOM LINE
Payton, defense push Falcons into oblivion

KEY PLAY
Willie Gault's back-to-back 20- and 50-yard receptions from Steve Fuller. They brought the ball to the 1-yard line, and from there William Perry scored.

KEY STAT
The defense held Atlanta to minus-22 yards passing and had five sacks.

Dallas, Perry took to the air this time after Steve Fuller had hit Willie Gault on consecutive passes of 20 and 50 yards. The touchdown was Perry's third of the season, second by rushing.

Normally sturdy fullback Matt Suhey hurt his back in the first half, and former Illini Calvin Thomas didn't miss a beat filling in. His 18-yard

The Falcons Gerald Riggs (42) gets a dose of heavy coverage by Chicago Bears defenders Mike Singletary (50), Dave Duerson (22), and Steve McMichaels, during first-half NFL action on November 24, 1985, in Chicago (above). Walter Payton is out of reach and off on a 40-yard touchdown run, part of a 102-yard day (right).

LESLIE FRAZIER
No. 21, cornerback

"I came in town for the first time in a while for the Bears convention, and I could not believe the way the fans treated myself and the other guys who played in the Super Bowl. It was almost like we just won it this past February."

"When we were walking off the field at halftime and they were playing 'The Super Bowl Shuffle,' it was almost like it was a home field for us."

"As far as I'm concerned, Walter Payton was the greatest running back ever. But a great human being who really tried to reach out to me and other young players and tried to be a good example."

"The scheme that we ran was so unique at the time. It took a lot of pressure off our defensive backs. People thought we were under a lot of pressure because we played so much man and we blitzed so much, but Buddy Ryan would tell us, 'Just cover them an extra second, Leslie, and we'll get there,' and boy, we usually got there."

"I don't think I would have that Super Bowl ring if not for Mike Ditka. Without question. When he came in, I don't know if we really understood what it took to win in the National Football League, the sacrifice that was necessary, the importance of teamwork. He instilled that toughness that we needed to get over the hump."

"Next to us winning a Super Bowl and meeting some of the guys I met, that period of time coaching at Trinity College was probably the greatest period of my life. To come in there and start a football program at 28 years of age and be an African American head coach at a Christian college was a great time."

"The birth of my kids and the lady I married—those are experiences I wouldn't change for anything in the world." ■

chapter XIV

Cannons Don't Fall out of Trees

It was on to New Orleans for Super Bowl XX.

The Bears' opponent was the New England Patriots, who had won the AFC championship by upsetting the Dolphins 31–14 in Miami. That score was a shocker, but Pats quarterback Tony Eason had been remarkably efficient in the game, completing 10 of 12 passes for three touchdowns. The Bears had beaten the Patriots 20–7 in the second game of the season, as everyone distantly recalled. It seemed like years ago. And in truth, over four months had gone by since that hot day at Soldier Field. Teams change. They learn, they peak, they flourish, they wane. There are injuries. Luck grows. It runs out. But the Bears could not fear the Patriots. The wreckage they had just caused in the playoffs was unprecedented. Nobody had tossed two shutouts before. Fear the Pats? As much as they feared Pat the Bunny.

Ditka had warned his team about getting complacent, however. He didn't want the players getting caught up in the hype. He didn't want them getting overwhelmed. He wanted them even-keeled, in their fashion. He quoted what his former Dallas Cowboys teammate Duane Thomas had once said to Super Bowl reporters: "If this is the ultimate game, why do they play one next year?"

"I had told all the guys from the beginning of the year that the only thing that would be acceptable to me, to all of us, was to win the Super Bowl." —Ditka on 1985

Before the Bears actually traveled to New Orleans, however, they visited the now-completed bubble in Champaign, Illinois, staying for a week of pre-New Orleans intensity on the University of Illinois campus. They had things to work on, because everyone said the Patriots had improved since the start of the year. Well, they had to improve. Indeed, the Pats finished up leading the AFC in takeaways with 47 and then got a stunning 16 more in their three playoff games. On offense Eason had been hurt in the sixth game, and the offense was handed to veteran quarterback Steve Grogan. New England had flourished under Grogan, winning its next six games, before Grogan himself was injured. Eason took over the starting role once more, but the Patriots did not falter under him this time. They continued on with their improved running game and an opportunistic, attacking defense.

The Bears tuned their defense in Champaign and set in motion Ditka's plan for offensive attack: be aggressive, take chances, be prepared to use Payton as a decoy if the Patriots made stopping him their sole focus. Whatever—never make the same mistake as in last year's NFC Championship Game. Do not sit back and let things happen. Make them happen.

Buddy Ryan was rumored to have been talking with the Philadelphia Eagles about their head coaching position, but he denied it. "I'm more excited about getting ready for the Super Bowl," he said. "That's what my mind's on right now."

Ryan's defense had finished the regular season ranked first in the NFL in turnovers, yards allowed, and points allowed. Everything that meant anything. "It would be an irreplaceable loss to this team," said Singletary of Ryan's possible departure. "It would take a long time to recover from his loss." The middle linebacker continued on in his somber, yet impassioned tone. "He's more than a coach. He's a leader, a father, and a friend."

Oh, and McMahon was injured once more. This time it was his lower back and upper buttocks. He was injured when he slid to the turf feet first in the Rams game, a signal for the defense to lay off, and still was steamrolled by a defender. "I got a serious pain in the ass right now," is how Jimmy Mac gently put it.

I was thinking about the class of 1983 when I looked at this team, all the rookies who joined the team in what was my second year as coach. That was some year for our draft. Eight of the guys we picked were starters—Jim Covert, Willie Gault, Dave Duerson, Tom Thayer, Richard Dent, Mark Bortz, Mike Richardson, and Dennis McKinnon. I mean, those are good players. You can say what you want about coaching and schemes and all that, but you need the horses to run the race. Ask any coach at the elite level, and if he's truthful, he'll say, "Yeah, we had the studs." We had ours. I'm the first to admit it. I had the best football players on the best team I'd ever seen. We went off to New Orleans feeling confident, to say the least.

I had told all the guys from the beginning of the year that the only thing that would be acceptable to me, to all of us, was to win the Super Bowl. It was a progression that we had to hold to. Develop a good team, develop the offense, the defense, develop the bonds, the teamwork, move forward, and when we got there, grab it all. Coming close would mean nothing now. We had been close. And I looked at that Dolphins game, that 38–24 loss. They weren't better than us. We stunk that day. I would have loved to have played them in the Super Bowl, to kick their ass, just to show everybody. But the Patriots beat them before we

got a chance. So what can you do?

That *Monday Night* game haunted me, to be honest. Miami couldn't have beaten us unless we didn't adjust to their offense. They weren't a better team than we were. I salute them for beating us, but they weren't nearly as good as we were. We had to do nothing to compensate for their offense for them to win. And we did nothing. I'll tell Buddy Ryan that, I'll tell anybody that. I'll go to my grave saying we played stupid defensive football.

What we did now was, we got all our work accomplished in Champaign. We studied and prepared and ran our drills, and we had our game plan laid out like a map. It was something I learned when I was with the Cowboys. I learned it from Tom Landry. Dallas went to a lot of Super Bowls, and there had always been two weeks between the NFC Championship Game and the final game. Tom put everything in that was needed in week one. He said then when you get down there you can tune it, you can tweak it. But you don't rebuild it. Super Bowl weeks are crazy enough. Why try to fight it? I mean, you know who the other team is, what they do. They've just done it for 18 games. They're not suddenly going to turn into something they've never been. You can get into a lot of trouble by trying to reinvent the wheel.

You know your players. You believe in what you've been doing. They believe in it. When we finally packed up and flew to New Orleans we had the right philosophy and the right feeling, and we never changed a damn thing once we got there.

We were not all perfect friends, don't get me wrong. As I may have mentioned, I don't believe Hampton and McMahon ever got along very well. They never really had a love for each other, and I don't know why that is. They were both the same

Jim McMahon ever cared more about himself than about the team. He did some strange things to draw attention to himself, but it never affected his teammates or his play.

There we were on our way to the Super Bowl, and naturally, stuff was happening everywhere. Again, I wasn't paying much attention to anything outside of the team and the preparation. McMa-

"McMahon, I think what you have to understand about him—whether you love him or hate him—is that he was one of the most competitive people on the planet."—Ditka on McMahon

kind of player, they just played on opposite sides of the ball. Dan gave everything he had, every down, every breath. He had knee problems and he was always beaten up, but it never stopped him. That's why he's in the Hall of Fame. McMahon, I think what you have to understand about him— whether you love him or hate him—is that he was one of the most competitive people on the planet. He wasn't acting like somebody he wasn't. If we were losing, you might have thought he was an egomaniac. But I can honestly say I don't think

hon had been on David Letterman, then Bob Hope, Fridge was doing stuff, everybody wanted Payton, there were posters. The damned "Super Bowl Shuffle" never ended. But I was worried a bit about Stanley Morgan, one of the Patriots' wide receivers. He may have been 30 years old, but he had the highest yards-per-reception average of any active NFL player, almost 21 yards a catch. He didn't catch a million balls, only 39 during the season, but he was dangerous as hell when he did.

Then there was their other wideout, a young

guy named Irving Fryar. Yeah, the media was watching us, and I suppose we gave them a lot to watch. But Fryar was getting watched, too. He'd missed the AFC Championship Game because he'd badly cut his ring finger and sliced the tendon in the little finger of his right hand. The news stories said he'd been in a fight with his pregnant wife and there was a knife, and, well, something happened. Besides catching passes, he was New England's leading punt returner. Hell, he was the leading punt returner in the NFL. Their safety Roland James replaced him against the Dolphins and fumbled twice. And a guy named Stephen Starring had replaced Fryar at wideout, and he didn't have a catch in the game. It mattered a bit to us whether Fryar played or not. Although, with our defense, maybe not that much.

New England coach Raymond Berry came out with some nice coach-speak. "I'm not sure that Starring isn't every bit as good as Fryar," he said.

Good work, Ray.

The main thing was, in my mind, Tony Eason was not Dan Marino. Raymond Berry is one of my favorite friends, a guy I respect and love to death. But Don Shula had realized before that 13th game that our offense was what it was, maybe he thought he could stop it. Maybe not. But the

Dolphins weren't terribly worried about our offense, at any rate. It was our defense that terrified them. So Shula went after it. He spent his time trying to beat our defense. Why could he do that? Because he had Dan Marino. Guys like Marino don't fall out of trees. Dan Marino has a cannon that God hands out to maybe one person a century. And he didn't give one to Tony Eason.

I told the players again about Duane Thomas and the Super Bowl. As a player I sat near Duane in the Dallas locker room, and I didn't know him well—he was real hard to understand and be a tight friend with. He was aloof and silent a lot. But he was a lot smarter than I thought.

Here's hoping we could be smart, too. ■

Chicago 24, Miami 38
One and Only: Season Smudged

Nobody's perfect, not even the 1985 Bears. When Miami had polished off the 38–24 victory that turned out to be the only blemish on the Bears' season, the Dolphins ensured that their 1972 record of 14–0 in the regular season and 17–0 overall would remain unequaled.

Seven seconds into the second quarter, the Bears trailed 17–7. Scoring on every first-half possession, Miami extended its lead to 31-10 at intermission. Mike Ditka chose to get into a shootout with the great Dan Marino in the first half, and Marino won. He wound up throwing for 270 yards and three touchdowns. Walter Payton, meanwhile, did not carry the ball until the Bears were behind 10–7 and nearly 10 minutes had elapsed.

One semi-highlight: Payton broke the NFL record with his eighth consecutive 100-yard game, but only because the Bears called timout three times on defense in the final minute after Payton had fumbled the ball away when he was stuck on 98 yards. But the Dolphins failed to run out the clock, and Payton got another chance, finishing with 121 yards.

"Walter Payton is the greatest football player to ever play the game," Ditka said. "Other people who call themselves running backs can't carry his jersey."

Jim McMahon had missed the previous three weeks with a tender shoulder, but he looked sharp in warmups. Still, Ditka left him on the bench until Steve Fuller sprained his ankle early in the fourth quarter. McMahon moved the Bears briefly until

Steve Fuller is helped from the field after spraining his ankle.

the sideline. But Ditka was calm, even cocky, postgame: "Nobody's perfect, and we proved it. Now it's what you do with it. Do you bounce back? We'll be back. [The Dolphins] deserved to win and we didn't. I hope they go as far as we're going to go and we play them again."

Of course, the Dolphins did not go to the Super Bowl. But the next day several Bears did record "The Super Bowl Shuffle." Perfect season or not, this team had swagger. ■

Chicago 24, Miami 38
DEC. 2, 1985, AT THE ORANGE BOWL

BOTTOM LINE
Dolphins pile it on right from the start

KEY PLAY
Maury Buford's punt being blocked at the Bears' 6-yard line. Nat Moore's ensuing touchdown made it 31–10 Miami, still in the first half.

KEY STAT
The Dolphins' 31 first-half points were the most against the Bears since the 1972 season opener.

throwing an interception with 6:12 to go. It was Miami's third interception against a team that had thrown just nine during its 12–0 start.

Not all the action was on the field. When the Bears gave up their fourth touchdown in the first half after a blocked punt at their own 6-yard line, Ditka screamed in frustration at Buddy Ryan on

The Miami Dolphins' Nat Moore (89) catches a Dan Marino pass and runs for a touchdown, December 2, 1985 (above). Linebacker Mike Singletary and the defense had no answer for Dan Marino and the Dolphins in the Bears' only defeat (right).

OTIS WILSON

No. 55, linebacker

"We had the '80s, and Michael had the '90s."

"When you say 'showmen,' we were just a crazy bunch of guys with great personalities, but when it was time to work, we went to work."

"With Buddy Ryan doing some of the things he did and Mike being vocal, hey, everybody was crazy."

"One thing Buddy said: 'If you don't know what you're doing, you'll be standing over here by me.' I couldn't stand him at first. No. 1, he wouldn't call us by our names. And he was on us so hard. But he wanted you to understand what was really going on. By my second year, it clicked in my head. I understood the total picture, and it made me a better player."

"'The Super Bowl Shuffle' sounded stupid. It sounded cocky. But, hey, we did it. We put ourselves out there in front of the bullet and made it happen. Willie Gault put that together, and Harold Washington was in office. They were trying to come up with an idea to raise money for various charities. That was the whole focus. It wasn't that we were trying to relate it to football. We were trying to raise money for charity. But it just turned out that way."

"[Mike] Singletary, an intense, smart individual. Hard-nosed. Almost like a coach on the field. Dedicated. Watching him study and understand the game helped me as well."

"Playing with Wilber [Marshall], I called him 'Pit Bull,' because he got on you and don't let you go."

"Dave Duerson and I, when we played, we'd get a little excited, a little carried away sometimes. We were just saying, 'We're like a pack of dogs out here.' We just started barking, and that's how it all started, believe it or not. I wish I could've put a patent on it. I'd be Bill Gates."

_____

"You couldn't double-team anyone on that line. If you double-team Richard [Dent], [Dan] Hampton and [Steve] McMichael would take your head off."

_____

"We saw something in everybody's eyes. We were coming, and they were like, 'Oh, Lord, here they come again.'"

_____

"The fans have always been great here in Chicago. Twenty-five years later, they can still name every player on that team. It's recognized, it's appreciated, and their support's always been great."

_____

"It's a brutal sport. You see this guy going into his fifth year, and this guy coming out of college is 21. I only have to pay him $20,000. I have to pay you a million. Which one do you think they're going to pay? You've got to look at all these things, kid. Don't go in there stupid."

_____

"Ed McCaskey used to always tell me, 'Otis, are you saving your money?' I'd say, 'Yes, I'm saving my money. I'm saving for a rainy day. I'm investing it wisely.' Then I'm saying in my mind, 'Because I'm not getting enough of it.' ■

chapter XV

Stick a Needle in This

The circus packed its tents, herded the giraffes and tigers onto the flatcars, rousted up the fat man and the bearded ladies and the jugglers and the strongmen, and headed down to New Orleans. There had been other eccentric and entertaining, even evil or nearly sanctified, teams in the 19 previous Super Bowls, but there had never been a carnival like the Chicago Bears. You had dark Raiders and sanctified Cowboys in the past. But here was something for everyone all on the same train.

From the riveting talent of Walter Payton to the intensity of the defensive line to the pulpit frenzy of Mike Singletary to the splendor of William "The Refrigerator" Perry to the antisocial unpredictability of Jim McMahon, there was everything on the Bears—you could observe it for hours and still have room for popcorn. And in the end it was all because there had never been a head coach like Mike Ditka.

Ditka's zeal was renowned, but whoever thought the wild man from western Pennsylvania would lead a band of disparate souls to the pinnacle of team sports? It was fascinating to all to know that Ditka was behind this thing, not as a player but as a coach. See how people could change? Or maybe change wasn't necessary, only tweaking, only passion. Ditka seemed so unlike Hank Stram or Chuck Noll or Bill Walsh or, of course, Tom Landry, as to be another species. But maybe not.

"Back then, Chicago teams always seemed to crumble when they were close to winning it all. The 1969 Cubs had done it, then the 1984 Cubs did. The White Sox blew the Series in 1959." —Ditka

McMahon's butt was still sore, of course, and he wanted his acupuncturist, a fellow named Hiroshi Shiriashi, to be flown to New Orleans to stick pins in his posterior. This created a minor brouhaha and much debate in the media and rowdy sports bars about the benefits of and philosophy behind Eastern healing processes. Ditka didn't care if somebody stuck a bazooka up McMahon's ass. If it calmed the quarterback down, eased his discomfort, and helped him play, do it. Willie Gault, ever the avant garde health savant, wanted the acupuncturist brought in, too, to work on him.

Shortly after the ruckus began, Bears president Michael McCaskey, who had barred the acupuncturist from flying on the team's charter plane, said fine, enough, I give. "We're going to welcome him with a brass band," McCaskey, the foppish chief, said sarcastically. Shiriashi and another specialist were flown to the bayou by the Illinois State Acupuncture Association—hey, this was where the publicity was!—and the needles came out.

McMahon himself was peeved with the press, *generally, telling the assembled masses on Media Monday at the Superdome that the stupid scrutiny "comes with winning. I don't think too many of you guys are up in Green Bay right now." He may have casually stuffed another gob of tobacco into his lower lip as he said this.*

Back in Chicago Mayor Harold Washington declared that the Daley Center Plaza was now "Bears Plaza," and had workers erect an electronically complex 600-square-foot television screen, consisting of 28,000 tiny tubes, that showed—what else?—the "Super Bowl Shuffle" on a continual loop. Folks everywhere lapped up the midwinter zaniness.

William Perry was asked about women fans, whether they wrote to him, maybe sent photos? "I don't get no letters from no ladies," Fridge declared sternly. Steve McMichael told the media about clearing out biker bars with Dan Hampton, about whatever deranged things came to his crafty mind. Asked by reporters about his snake-hunting hobby, how he lured the snakes, McMichael drawled for their amusement, "You throw a reporter out there, and when the rat-

tlesnake bites, you just grab it behind the neck."

Pete Rozelle declared of the Bears, speaking for the universe, or at least the TV-aware NFL, "We love them. They got a 75 rating for the Rams game."

The Bears were on the cover of Time *magazine. They were officially the rage.*

The truth is we were nervous and concerned, but we also were confident as hell. As Dennis McKinnon told the media, if we don't make mistakes, there's no way in hell the Patriots can beat us. That was just the plain truth. Hampton said we didn't want to squeak by, we wanted to beat them soundly. And we did want to. We were favored by 10 points or something, but I thought that if we did what we were capable of, we could win big, really make a statement.

Otis Wilson even said we wanted a shutout. Fine. We did. But let's not talk too much. Their guy Raymond Clayborn said he thought Wilson "was crazy," and he added, "Obviously, it will be an incentive for our offense to prove them wrong. And I know they will." Clayborn played defensive back. I don't think he knew much about our defense. He'd never played against it. I think he should have asked, oh, let's say the Giants or Rams about it. But that was fine. Who cared about Raymond Clayborn? It was all just talk.

There was a flu bug going around down in New Orleans, and I don't just mean from Bourbon Street hangovers. Tony Eason had a case of it, Kevin Butler missed Friday's practice and was hospitalized because of it, and some coaches and other people didn't feel too hot. But this was the biggest game of most people's lives, so, I mean, are you going to miss it because of a virus?

There were people coming and telling me they saw McMahon out on Bourbon Street at 2:30 in the morning. And, no, I didn't have a curfew until Saturday, the night before the game. But we had wakeup calls at 6:30 in the morning, and if the guys didn't know what was really important just now, they were pretty messed up.

Back then, Chicago teams always seemed to crumble when they were close to winning it all. The 1969 Cubs had done it, then the 1984 Cubs did. The White Sox blew the Series in 1959. The Bears had that 1963 NFL championship, the one I played on, but that was 22 years previous, and it wasn't the Super Bowl. Getting close didn't mean jack to me. You practice and work so you can get close. Then you take close and you kick its carcass to hell. You want the top, the championship. You smell it, you taste it. You get it. That's all there is.

McMahon's acupuncture guy showed up, and Jim and Willie got worked on. Got stuck with more pins than a voodoo doll, I guess. The press asked me about McMahon's butt on Wednesday, and I said it was 200 percent better. Was it? I don't know. Jesus, I was supposed to be monitoring his ass?

I just knew he was going to play. I mean, McMahon even wore a headband that said, "ACUPUNCTURE" on it. I just hoped everyone would make it to game time. McMahon supposedly had pushed a photographer who was trying to take his picture in the French Quarter. Now that I think about it, maybe I did impose a curfew after that. But I wasn't going around and knocking on guys' doors.

Myself, I wasn't partying. I got a touch of the

People were asking about the weather, and if it might affect us. We're playing in a freaking dome! Honest to God, that happened. Then on Wednesday a helicopter flies over when we're practicing outdoors at the New Orleans Saints' practice field in Metairie, Louisiana. It hovers overhead, taking photos or whatever, and next thing you know, McMahon has dropped his shorts and is mooning the camera crew, showing them his hurt butt cheeks. Next day in the papers, there he is, doing his thing. What can I say? *Shame on you?* Yes, I cared, because I thought it was an embarrassment

"I was thinking constantly that two teams get to these championships and nobody remembers the team that loses." —Ditka

flu and took it easy at night. I really didn't feel too well the whole week. My parents were in town, and we went out to dinner one night, Diana and my folks, but that was about it. My kids were there, too. I waited in the Hilton Hotel is all I did. Otis, meanwhile, was still talking, but that's because the press kept asking questions. I think they'd ask dumb-ass questions until they took their last little breath. "The Rams are better than the Patriots," Otis told them. "I don't think there's any comparison." There probably wasn't.

to the organization. People would look at us and say we're idiots. Maybe we were to a degree. But I wouldn't call attention to the fact. Jim was wrong there. A little discretion might be in order. I wasn't thrilled. But would I go to the wall for him as my starting quarterback? Absolutely.

For us as a team, the main thing was we never changed our philosophy in New Orleans. It started in Platteville, and we believed in what we were doing. You don't take risks if you don't have to, but if you don't risk something, you have no chance.

Gary Fencik Remembers '85

Super Bowl QBs: McMahon's Butt, Tony Eason's Fear

"We made it down there to New Orleans and we're the Bears, so it's a wild time. McMahon's butt was an unusual injury, in that it was a bad contusion. That was a wow! All those acupuncture needles and stuff, I don't know. But the scariest thing to me was Tom Thayer getting shots in his fingers in a huddle.

"The game takes its toll. I remember Tony Eason in the Super Bowl, and I'd never seen a quarterback like him. We'd played the Patriots earlier in the season, so Eason knew what was coming. Only worse. He was not looking downfield. He was not looking for open receivers. He was looking for a place to duck. I could see that, and I could see all the emotion in the huddle from the defensive line. I'd been in the league 10 years, and I wanted to enjoy this, to savor it.

"Years later I ran into Lions quarterback Joe Ferguson at a golf outing, and as soon as I got there he let it be known he did not want to talk about the hit Wilber Marshall put on him, under the chin, the one that knocked him out while he was still in mid-air. He did not want to talk about that.

"I guess I can understand that. What we did to people wasn't much fun for them. Though I must say, it was quite a fun time for us."

We risked being aggressive. That's what we were. That's what we would remain.

The night before the game we had meetings. Basically, that's it. I met with the whole team, and I told them you're not winning this game for me or for Halas or McCaskey or anybody else. You're winning it for yourselves, for the guy sitting next to you. It's not about anything I've ever said. You have this wonderful moment in time, and you can answer to each other forever.

I had some of the guys stand up and say what the game meant to them. We broke it up then and I talked to the offense, and Buddy talked to the defense in another room. I guess their part got pretty crazy. They might have gone nuts. There was a lot of noise, and I think maybe a film projector got smashed and maybe there were some holes in the wall. I think Buddy told the players he loved them and he was leaving, taking that Eagles job. I don't know for sure. But that's what he told me later. And they knew something was over, this was it. Their general had one more battle. The defense had its bayonettes fixed. I know that.

I went to bed early. Sunday was a blur. With a game starting so late, it was like a *Monday Night* game, and that just messes with you. All day long you have to wait around. And here we are so close to the Superdome that we can walk there. No need to leave early or anything. I know I got up around

5 AM or earlier, and we had Mass for the Catholics and devotionals for the Protestants, and we got the position coaches together for a while. But it was really nothing. We try to eat our pregame meal three or four hours before game time, so we did that, but I don't remember many details. It's all such a cloud of anticipation. I do know I was thinking constantly that two teams get to these championships, and nobody remembers the team that loses.

That's crazy, if you think about it.

We're 17–1, but if we finish 17–2, it's nothing. I had too much time to think. You get too much time, you get pregnant with ideas. But I had watched so much film of the Patriots, I knew the whole defense would key on Payton, and why not? So what a great weapon that was. And what a great decoy he could be.

The thing is our defense hadn't been scored on in the playoffs, and to say we were confident was an understatement. Still, you don't know. You don't know. You just don't know. The clock would not move.

After what seemed like years, the game finally started. Actually, it almost began, and then it was delayed a little bit because of too much smoke from the fireworks inside the Superdome or something. Noise, screaming, cameras everywhere. Everybody was uptight. Even McMahon. We got

the ball, and on the second play Jim called the wrong formation on a weak-side slant, and Walter got hit just when he was getting the ball and fumbled. The Patriots recovered at our 19-yard line. Oh, this is a great way to start. This is perfect.

McMahon had had his butt shot up by team doctor Clarence Fossier, probably with novocaine and a little cortisone in there. He also was wearing gloves. Indoors. Help me. He told me he was going to do that. He'd worn them in the last two games, which were cold as can be, but here it's 72 degrees, maybe hotter. I said, "Is that the right thing to do?"

"I get a better grip on the ball," he said.

"Okay," I said. "Do whatever you want."

But when he came to the sideline now, I said, "What are you doing?"

"I messed up," he said. "I called the wrong formation."

When he called a Slant 24, it should have gone left to the weak side, instead of to the right. Maybe he got confused for an instant by the numbers, because, see, I numbered even to the left and odd to the right, which nobody else does. That was from Coach Landry. . . .

But this is the thing—our defense didn't let New England move forward an inch after the turnover, not a single inch, and they had to settle for a field goal from the same spot. Talk about character. We had become a whole.

And the rout was on.

We scored the next 44 points. It was an ass-whipping. Plain and simple. Everything we knew we could do, we did. I don't think I've ever been prouder of a game plan in my life. They keyed on Walter like we thought they would, and so we used him in motion or flanked him or used him as a decoy and let Suhey carry the ball. We hit them with so many missiles it was unreal. The first time we got the ball back, we hit them with a 43-yard pass to Gault. I wasn't going to play it tight. I knew going in this was balls to the wall.

Butler had two field goals early, then Suhey scored on an 11-yard run. It was only 23–3 at the half, but we were killing them. They had minus-14 yards of total offense for the half. We were making them go backward.

In the third quarter we scored two touchdowns to make it 37–3. Then we had the ball at their 1, and I sent in Fridge. He plowed it over to make the score 44–3. I'd already put him in to block once and also to pass. That didn't work, and he got tackled while still looking to throw. He is probably the heaviest man ever to be sacked.

Tony Eason, I'm not blaming him, but I think our defense was so relentless that he got shell-shocked. I think he started looking for the rush, for who was going to earhole him or hit his back or his knees or slam him, and he couldn't concentrate on routes or receivers. I mean, wow, he did not complete a single pass in the game. He was zero-for-eight, oh for the Super Bowl. Steve Grogan came in later, but it was history. We annihilated the Patriots 46–10. Richard Dent was the MVP, and that was a great choice. He represented that incredible defense.

McMahon played well after that first series, with two touchdown runs and 256 yards passing. He wore all of these headbands, too, looked like a street sign, but he was very clever about it. One said "Plato" or "Pluto" or something like that, for a friend of his, one was for juvenile diabetes, and one said "POW-MIA" for the war veterans. Not that I was watching his forehead. But this, I found out later, was famous stuff. This was what got the media excited.

When it was over, when the final second ran off, I felt this incredible sense of relief. The hype and the buildup had been so huge that I just felt totally drained. I didn't even notice the guys coming to pick me up. Some players grabbed Buddy and hoisted him up, and two guys got me. Looking at photos now, I see it was McMichael with my right leg and Fridge with my left. It scared me a bit, to tell you the truth. I'd never been lifted like that before. My hips and legs aren't in mint condition, you know. But it was a great feeling, too. Two defensive players were picking me up, although

"Life is fragile. You never know. My buddy and teammate Joe Marconi died young. You wonder why some go and some stay." —Ditka

Fridge was part of the offense, too, of course. As I recall, they were very gentle.

I was glad I got to have some fun with William Perry. I did the stuff with him, because he was a good player and I liked him. I was going to have him run for a touchdown, catch one, and throw one. It almost worked. I probably would have let him kick a field goal, too. Nah, I wouldn't have. I wouldn't have let Walter kick one. There were limits. People said I told William, "I made you a hero," but I never said that. We just had a good time, that's all.

But what I realized after the game, after we were champions, 18–1, and bigshots of the day, was that Walter Payton didn't score in the game. And that bothered him. And because it bothered him, it bothered me. McMahon had two short TD runs. Perry had one. Suhey had one. Walter had none. I didn't plan that. That put a damper on things later. I asked Walter, and he said it didn't bother him, but it did. I regret not giving him that honor. But we had a game plan, and he was the whole reason it worked, because wherever he went, the Patriots defense went. Later I explained this to him. I don't think he ever accepted it totally.

The other thing I regret is Les Frazier blowing out his knee on a reverse on a punt return. He was a defensive back and used to running backward. Now he's carrying the ball, going forward? I love Steve Kazor, our special teams coach, but I don't know if that all was necessary. It was a freak thing, but Les was never really the same afterward.

I mean, think about it. A bench kid named Keith Ortego—a guy wearing my No. 89, by the way—signals a fair catch and then grabs the ball and runs and hands off to Les. There's a penalty flag, and the play doesn't even count. Frazier was one of the best cornerbacks in the NFL, and he'll never get credit for it, because he didn't have a long career, and he wasn't a showboat like Deion Sanders. And at his highest peak, at our moment of glory, he goes down like that. I guess that's football.

Life is fragile. You never know. My buddy and teammate Joe Marconi died young. You wonder why some go and some stay. Why do things happen? It was so good for Marconi, then boom—dead at 54. Everybody knows about the tragedy of Brian Piccolo. And I am always haunted by Farrington and Galimore in that crash.

You have to appreciate things at the moment and never stop trying to achieve what you want. A while back I read that a guy I played against, Jim Otto, had his leg amputated. He never missed a game in 15 years, but he's had over 50 major surgeries because of his injuries, and he has so many artificial joints that his body's immunity to infection is about gone. It's a tragedy. It's like old George Connor of the Bears who went through stuff like that.

Jim Otto was a warrior. Back then we played hurt. Sports medicine sure wasn't what it is now. And you didn't want to have your job taken from you, the way Wally Pipp got his taken by Lou Gehrig. See, you get in the starting blocks and you run the race. That's what you do. That's what George Connor did. That's life. You can't rewrite things as you go along. You have to go straight ahead on the path you've chosen, with all your might. Who is Jim Otto? All those things. That's who he is.

And yet I'm working on getting a better shake from the NFL for the retired veterans. A lot of them, more each day, are in bad shape. The dementia from brain trauma is without a doubt the worst problem. And the guys without money suffer the most.

Me, I wouldn't change anything. I had that groin problem, and they shot me up all the time with cortisone back in the day, so deep it went to my hip socket, and I think that's why my hip wore out. They say you should get cortisone a couple times a year, tops, and I was getting two or three shots a week. And the dislocated foot I got when a guy fell on it back in the early 1960s, that caused a lot of other things to go. I remember Dr. Fox, the old Bears doctor, put it in a cast in training camp. But I'm "Iron Mike," so I'm out dancing every night. He takes the cast off after a month and he says, "That doesn't look very good." I take a step and fall down.

I don't think he did anything. I don't think he did anything but put a cast on it. Later a doctor said he could fix my foot, but he'd have to break about eight bones to do it. And I played the whole season on it. Never got it fixed. Fox is the guy who messed up Dick Butkus's leg, too. But I loved the guy. What the hell, I don't know. You didn't sue medical people back then. I sure wasn't going to. You're the player. He's the doctor. Play ball.

I was sorry about Todd Bell and Al Harris not being part of that Super Bowl season. But they got bad advice. In life, that happens. And it was true that Richard Dent was underpaid at $90,000. And he should be in the Hall of Fame, and I think he will be. But where else was he going to make that kind of money? And whether I'm right or wrong, this is about team. And we were a team. Who knows what would have happened if you go back and change a thing here or a thing there? Maybe if

Todd and Al had been on the team we wouldn't have won. That's why you do what you feel you have to do, with what you've got.

It's cold and it's cruel, this life. But it's great, too. It's all there together.

Take that movie I was in. There I am playing myself, smoking a cigar, and who's next to me? Why, it's Will Ferrell, one of the funniest guys in the world. He came to my bar one night and he did the greatest Harry Caray you've ever heard. Diana and I were dying. And who's on the other side? Why, it's Robert Duvall, who may be a better actor even than Robert DeNiro. Why me with these guys? I don't know. Nobody knows.

• • • • •

So there we were, champions of the world. Maybe I thought about luck a little when I popped my head up through the sunroof of that limo, there in downtown Chicago. How lucky I've been. But damn, it was cold. Beautiful, in a frozen way. What a place for a parade, especially one that wasn't moving.

I hadn't slept much, but that wind was a nice slap to the face. All those thousands and thousands of people cheering. It was wonderful. And yet, on Tuesday, less than 48 hours after we won, the space shuttle blew up. That put things in perspective. We didn't visit the White House like we were supposed to because of that. We were about the only winning Super Bowl team that never got to do that.

But for one moment in time, one fleeting second, we were the best in the world. In that moment we were the best of all, because we had beaten down our opponents, fair and square. And if you don't play to beat the best, to beat them all, why play?

I can say I came full circle. I feel like I started in Chicago with the Bears and George Halas, and I came back and did what I wanted to and lived up to his legacy. I'm not sure the Old Man could appreciate the significance of what him trusting me meant to me. Maybe he saw that I was a lot like him. That sounds funny even saying it. He was probably more serious than I was. I messed around a little, you know.

But that Super Bowl XX win stands alone in Chicago history. An ass-whupping. Pure and simple. It's like what columnist Bob Verdi wrote: "The New England Patriots were lucky to escape with their Boston accents intact."

Me, I thought somebody just invented this giant merry-go-round, and we were getting on, and we were going to ride forever. And it would be fun.

Then it all sort of ended. We continued for a while, but Buddy left to coach Philadelphia and jealousies came into play, and Wilbur Marshall went to Washington, and McMahon got hurt, and people said I did too many commercials and on and on. I've heard it all.

But I didn't change as a coach. I couldn't. It's

Gary Fencik Remembers '85

Super Bowl Musings

"I've been taken out of a game earlier, but I don't recall when. In Super Bowl XX, I didn't play in the fourth quarter, so the release, the realization came on the sideline while the game was going on. We had time to observe and to celebrate, to soak it all in on the sideline rather than the locker room. Everybody played. Les Frazier ran a reverse on a punt and blew his knew out, a crazy play. No excuses. Every week you gotta be ready to play. And there on the sideline we had fifteen minutes to appreciate what we'd done, to pretty much get the disbelief out of us.

"That Miami game in Week 13, the loss to Marino and Shula, that game that kept us from going undefeated, got us back on track. The previous two weeks nobody had scored on us, and then McMahon got hurt and it all went wrong on us. A long pass was deflected off Dent's hand for a long completion and touchdown—that kind of bad luck. 'It ain't gonna happen this week,' we sensed. But it was a great thing for the Bears, got us re-focused.

"Then the next day we did the 'Super Bowl Shuffle.' It was all for charity and we were told we could change our words if we wanted. 'It's Gary here/And I'm Mister Clean/They call me Hit Man/Don't know what they mean.' Those are quality, huh? At any rate we did the Shuffle, and poor Steve Fuller has a bad ankle, and he's on stage and he can't move at all, so he's a little uncool. I don't know if we ever made any money on this. But I also didn't know it was going to be a video and that it would haunt me for the rest of my natural life."

my essence. The people who say outside stuff interfered with my drive are full of crap. I'm an emotional person. I get wrapped up in things. And I wanted this to go on and on. But it didn't, and no Bears team has won the Super Bowl since. The Patriots, whom we hammered that day, have won three Super Bowls in the last 10 years. I didn't think the Bears would go a quarter-century without repeating, I really didn't. I guess we were kind of living a fairy tale back in the day.

It hurts me that the Bears haven't won the championship again. There are a lot of reasons why they haven't, and I could tell you a lot of stuff. But that's for another day.

Besides, I don't get mad at things any more. Not things I can't control. Not life. Really, I don't. I only get mad at cab drivers now and then.

Because they're idiots. ■

Chicago 17, Indianapolis 10
Ugly, but They'll Take It

Turns out meaningless games were not meaningless to championship-starved Soldier Field fans, who showered a 12–1 team with boos at halftime of a listless effort against Indianapolis. The Bears already had clinched home-field advantage throughout the playoffs but no longer could go undefeated, so they lacked motivation for the final three games the schedule said they had to play. Still, a 17–10 victory was better than the reverse.

Predictably, the Bears came out flat. Problem was, they stayed that way until a couple of time-consuming drives in the second half stuck the Colts on the shelf.

Jim McMahon returned from sick bay and started for the first time in five weeks. He said his shoulder felt fine, but he was nothing special with an 11-of-23 afternoon for 145 yards and no touchdowns.

Walter Payton came through late in the third quarter to break a 3–3 halftime tie with a 16-yard touchdown run.

Steady as ever, he extended his NFL record by gaining 100 yards for the ninth game in a row. He ran 20 times in the second half after only six in the first half because, coach Mike Ditka said, he "got nasty notes from the media saying, 'Run Payton.'"

Fighting the effects of the flu, Payton finished with 111 yards, yet he said his most satisfying moment had been "a block for Matt Suhey."

Actually, on a day devoid of big plays for the Bears, Calvin Thomas wound up scoring the

Leslie Frazier and Wilber Marshall join forces to stop Colts tight end Pat Beach.

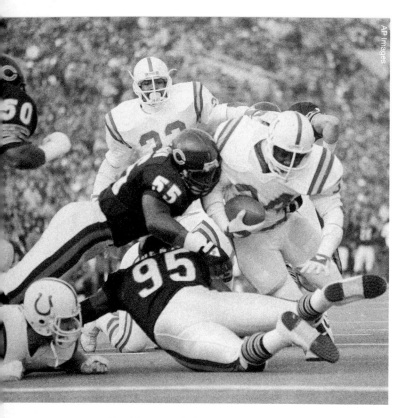

Maury Buford the day's most valuable player, as he booted terrific punts to the 4-yard line to set up both touchdowns.

"Wasn't fancy, but it's 13–1," said linebacker Otis Wilson, who recorded the Bears' only sack late in the game.

In the Bears' last home appearance before the playoffs, even a sluggish effort was enough to propel them to their 13th victory, which tied the franchise record set in 1934.

"I'm not unhappy," Ditka said. "I didn't think it would be a blowout like a lot of people. The main thing is we're going into the playoffs, and people are going to have to come here to play us."

After enduring this stinker, fans would say the playoffs could come none too soon. ∎

Chicago 17, Indianapolis 10
DEC. 8, 1985, AT SOLDIER FIELD

BOTTOM LINE
Sluggish Bears have enough to win eyesore

KEY PLAY
Walter Payton's 16-yard touchdown run late in the third quarter. He rushed for more than 100 yards for the ninth straight game.

KEY STAT
For the only time all season, the Bears had no takeaways or giveaways.

clinching touchdown on a three-yard scamper with six minutes left.

That offset an ensuing 61-yard Mike Pagel-to-Wayne Capers pass on which cornerback Mike Richardson got undressed.

The defense forced concern by failing to force a turnover for the first time all season. That made

Bears defenders Otis Wilson (55) and Richard Dent move in to bring down Indianapolis Colts halfback George Wonsley during the first quarter of the game in Chicago on December 8, 1985 (above). Richard Dent hovers over Indianapolis quarterback Mike Pagel after leveling him in the fourth quarter (right).

TOM THAYER
No. 57, guard

"It starts with Joliet Catholic and wanting to play football there, playing college football somewhere, and then always shooting for the stars, and shooting for the stars was the NFL, and the Bears were always a dream situation."

"The day we were announcing my USFL contract [with the Chicago Blitz], it was the same day as the NFL draft, and here I am, sitting in a room with George Allen, signing a contract so I can stay in Chicago, and after that announcement I drive home and pull into my driveway, and my sister says, 'Jim Finks is on the phone. The Bears just drafted you.' I kind of felt like I blew the opportunity to live out every childhood dream in playing for your hometown team. But on the positive end of it, I signed a three-year contract, and the Bears had my rights for four years."

"The best thing about 1985 was losing the coin toss and letting the defense go on the field first. Those guys usually set the tone."

"Ditka was great because he motivated by fear of losing your job. I think if you have any pride or any passion for the game of football, that's one of the best motivations you can have."

"Walter Payton was the toughest man I've ever known. He was physically fit and tough. If you go back and look at Walter's football helmet, he wore the old suspension helmet—the one that just has the belt around your head, the one that doesn't have that sophisticated pad system that they have today—and he never missed a game with a head injury. He never left a game because he had a concussion."

"Every time I think of Fridge, I smile."

"I think Keith Van Horne was as smart about our offense as our quarterbacks were."

"Super Bowl XX, I was so young in my NFL career that I expected it to happen again. You hear people talk about, 'Oh, you should've won it two or three more times.' Maybe not, but at least one more time."

"For me, as an ex-Bear and as a Chicago resident, I get frustrated going to opponents' stadiums

and talking to different people involved with different teams, and they don't have that fear of the Bears coming. There's no respect for the Bears' swagger."

"I think it's my Type-A personality. Surfing in Hawaii is the best thing I've ever done since I quit playing football. When you pull up to the ocean

and you look out and you see that the surf is 10 feet, that puts the same nervousness in your stomach that you felt before kickoff. I think that's healthy for me."

"What am I proudest of? Man, it sounds corny, but it's being able to experience everything in my professional life with my family." ■

Chicago 19, New York 6
Buddy System: Class in Session

Everyone knew that the Bears were dominating with their defense. But, ever the skeptic and bothered by mediocre performances the previous two games, coordinator Buddy Ryan turned classroom proctor. In the week leading up to the Jets game, Ryan gave his players three written tests on the game plan. It proved the value of cramming for finals. The Bears limited their 11th opponent to 10 or fewer points and allowed zero touchdowns for the fourth time as they hammered the Jets 19-6 in East Rutherford, N.J. Their stamp was clear when sizing up the Jets' third quarter. New York's five drives netted 0, 6, 2, 4, and 4 yards. "Our defense took the game away," Mike Ditka said.

Especially Richard Dent. The lanky defensive end punctuated that superior third quarter by climbing on the back of quarterback Ken O'Brien, at that time the NFL's leading passer, and knocking the ball out of his arm on sacks that ended consecutive possessions. Dent also abused New York left tackle Reggie McElroy so much that he was driven out of the game.

As the Bears won 14 games for the first time in franchise history, the offense was not outstanding. But in the cold, windy weather, it got the job done by controlling the ball for an incredible 39 minutes and 36 seconds. Tight end Tim Wrightman's first career touchdown reception and four field goals by Kevin Butler provided more than enough for the stellar defense. Butler's second field goal was his 26th of the season, breaking the club record Mac

Linebacker Jim Morrissey closes in to tackle a Jets receiver.

ended at nine after the Jets held him to 53 yards on 28 carries. New York stopped him for a loss or no gain 11 times. "They were the best defense we've faced," center Jay Hilgenberg said. Payton did catch a 65-yard pass that set up the field goal on which Butler passed Percival.

So the Bears went into a hostile city, played in nasty weather, contained a potent offense ... and weren't satisfied. "No question we've got to play better," Jim McMahon said. But how to stay motivated? Said defensive lineman Dan Hampton, "You don't need any motivation except pride." ■

Chicago 19, New York 6
DEC. 14, 1985, AT GIANTS STADIUM

BOTTOM LINE
Ryan's students get it right again

KEY PLAY
Jim McMahon's 65-yard pass against the wind to Walter Payton in the pivotal third quarter. It set up a Kevin Butler field goal that gave the Bears a 13–6 edge.

KEY STAT
Butler accounted for all but six points with field goals of 18, 31, 36, and 21 yards, plus an extra point.

Percival set in 1968. His last one broke Bob Thomas' team record of 11 in a row. That 21-yard chip shot came with just 17 seconds left in a contest that already had been decided, though Ditka denied he was rubbing it in. "We were just going for the record," he said.

However, Walter Payton no longer was going for a record. His streak of 100-yard rushing games

Tight end Emery Moorehead looks for running room after a catch (above). Chicago Bears quarterback Jim McMahon sits on his helmet while warming up for practice at the team's indoor training facility on December 10, 1985.

JAY HILGENBERG
No. 63, center

"We accepted it as an offensive line that if we win, all the credit's going to go someplace else, but if we lose, it's going to come at us."

———————

"We had a great defense, no doubt about it. The week of practice I'd have at Lake Forest a lot of times was harder than games."

———————

"But if you look at that season, the early games, teams were scoring some points on us. It took a few games for the defense to start shutting it down, but once they did, they were devastating to offenses."

———————

"The nice thing about Ditka is you always knew where you stood."

———————

"Head coaches, that's their role: they're supposed to yell and scream and do all that. When Ditka came in, he got rid of guys who were just happy being professional football players. He wanted professional football players who wanted to win. He changed the whole culture."

———————

"When he Jim McMahon was healthy, I tell you, he was into football more than anybody there was. He loved football. He was very smart at it. It was always nice to read the papers during training camp to see what was going on with him and Ditka. I remember being mad at Jim a couple times because all he was doing was getting Mike angry, and he'd take it out on us all the time."

———————

"When we went up to Lambeau and played the Packers, that was during the time where the quarterback didn't have to run a play if the crowd was too loud. We were on the 1-yard line going in, and McMahon was taunting the Packer fans, being really brutal. They were too loud, so he wasn't going to run the play. He was just taunting the Packer fans up there. Now, this is after the Monday night game, and they all know Fridge is going to get the ball. But this was the one where they faked the run

to Fridge and he went into the end zone and caught the pass for a touchdown. Just to hear Lambeau Field being so loud and McMahon's being difficult, and then hearing the quiet after Fridge caught a touchdown pass, we were just laughing so hard out there."

———————

"Walter Payton was the greatest. I remember the first play I was ever in on. We were going against a 3-4 defense. The nose guard threw me off, and Walter was running through the right tackle hole. I started getting back up on my feet, and I looked behind me. Remember watching as a kid the high step that Walter would do? It was just like I was a little kid watching him high-step right at me. I tried to get out of his way, but I just catch his knee with my shoulder, and he goes down. I thought, 'Man, my first play in the NFL, and I tackle Walter Payton.' Walter goes, 'Next time, just lay on the ground.'"

———————

"I remember Willie Gault on the plane after the Monday night loss in Miami asking me if I wanted to be in 'The Super Bowl Shuffle.' I said no. I didn't want any part of that. I said, 'Are you kidding me? We just got beat on national TV, and now we're going to go sing about being in the Super Bowl? Come on.'"

———————

"I was born in Iowa City in University Hospital, so I was a Hawkeye from Day One. My father was coaching at Iowa at the time. My dad grew up in Iowa, went to the University of Iowa, and in 1953 was a first-team All-American. My older brother Jim was first-team All-Big Ten and a two-time captain of Iowa. When he was a senior, I was a freshman at Iowa. Then when I was a senior, Joel was a freshman at Iowa. Joel went on to play 10 years with the Saints. We were all centers. My uncle Wally was an All-American football player at Iowa and played for the Vikings. He started four Super Bowls with the Vikings." ■

Chicago 37, Detroit 17
Many Stars of This Show

On paper, a 20-point victory over a division rival to end the regular season 15–1 would seem to provide a springboard into the playoffs. But these were the '85 Bears, who could find something wrong with a $100 bill. For instance, it took the Bears more than 46 minutes to score an offensive touchdown. They turned the ball over four times, three on interceptions and once on a fumble.

They managed just two touchdowns on eight trips inside the Detroit 30-yard line. They failed by four points to break the 1978 Pittsburgh Steelers' record for points allowed in a 16-game schedule, finishing with 198.

They watched inspirational leader Mike Singletary limp off the field with a sprained left knee.

Even though coach Mike Ditka berated his team after the victory at the Pontiac Silverdome, the Bears had become just the second squad in NFL history to win 15 games in the regular season and the first in a dozen years to go unbeaten in the NFC Central. They finished second in the league in points scored and first in total defense, first in rushing defense, and third in passing defense.

Many individuals merited notice, even the grouchy Ditka, who matched Bill Walsh as the only coaches with 15 wins in a season. The incomparable Walter Payton became the first man with more than 2,000 yards in combined rushing and receiving yardage three years in a row.

The first of Kevin Butler's three field goals gave him 134 points for the season and broke Gale

Dennis Gentry tightropes the sideline and holds the ball aloft at the end of his 94-yard kickoff return.

AP Images

that the Lions quarterback's arms dangled at his side before he hit the ground.

Laughter was provided in the fourth quarter when William Perry, who had forced James Jones to cough up the ball earlier in the game, scooped up a fumble and trudged some 40 hilarious yards downfield before being hauled down inside the Detroit 20. That set up Jim McMahon's 11-yard pass to Ken Margerum for the final touchdown of an irregular regular season.

Now the playoffs—and history—awaited. ■

Chicago 37, Detroit 17
DEC. 22, 1985, AT THE SILVERDOME

BOTTOM LINE
Lots of contributors help end on right note

KEY PLAY Dennis Gentry's 94-yard kickoff return for a TD to open the second half. The play helped turn a 6–3 lead into a rout.

KEY STAT The Bears recovered four Detroit fumbles and picked off three interceptions.

Sayers' NFL rookie scoring record set 20 years earlier. Ron Rivera, replacing the injured Singletary, became the 21st Bear to score by returning a recovered fumble five yards in the fourth quarter.

Dennis Gentry electrified his team by returning the second-half kickoff 94 yards for a touchdown that busted open a tight 6–3 contest. Wilber Marshall creamed Joe Ferguson so hard on a rollout

Bears' coach Mike Ditka autographs a football for a fan in Cicero, Illinois, on December 27, 1985 (above). Otis Wilson is an unpleasant backfield visitor, sacking Detroit's Eric Hipple (right).

DENNIS MCKINNON
No. 85, wide receiver

"The thing I'm proudest of was that I was part of a group of guys who did what they had to do, who gave Walter a chance to be in a place he should've always been. He was the quintessential icon. I was humbled by his presence."

_____

"Even today, there's not a day that goes by that I don't think about Walter Payton. I still say that this city has not honored him the way he should be. No different than the National Football League. We hope to change that. We would love to be able to get the National Football League on one given Sunday that a percentage of all tickets sold in all the markets goes to the Walter Payton Fund, which is something that has never been done, not even in our own backyard."

_____

"Having the great Payton, we were a running team. Everybody talks about how great our defense was, but it's ironic that we led the league in time of possession, second in the league in scoring, three consecutive years I think we led the league in rushing, which means the defense was definitely rested."

"Our offense, we never wanted to sit on the bench. We wanted to stand and see what quarterback would get knocked out. There was always a bounty on every quarterback."

_____

"We were so disappointed that we didn't get the Dolphins. We never believed the Patriots had a prayer anyway."

_____

"Opening lineup. We're in the tunnel. They're doing the introductions, and they said, "No. 85, from Florida State, Dennis McKinnon." Here I am, in my third year in the league, a free-agent walk-on, has a chance to start at a place I never thought I would be. It's remarkable when you look back on it."

_____

"Yeah, I complained. Yeah, I was screaming, 'Willie's not open. I am. Throw me the ball. What do I have to do? Who else do I have to knock out?'"

_____

"The McKinnon payoff? At a time where if you were really good at returning kicks, teams didn't kick it to you. A majority of our guys who were on

special teams weren't making a whole lot of money. I wanted to insure my safety. I would always tell whoever makes the block that springs me, there's $5,000 or $10,000 for you."

"[Mike Ditka] is a guy in my first year I couldn't stand. I got yelled at every single practice as a rookie. He had me learning three different positions—flanker, split end, tight end. Then I had veteran players tell me the wrong plays because they didn't want to practice. I was frustrated, frustrated, frustrated. Then I realized that he saw something in me that some people didn't see."

"We did something so special to this town because we played for a city. We didn't just play for the Bears or for the McCaskeys. We played for the city of Chicago. For every Bear fan who got off a plane in any city, they were proud to be from Chicago." ■

Chicago 21, New York 0
Knocked Cold

After shutting down the defending champion 49ers in the wild-card playoff game, the New York Giants believed they had a chance against the Bears in the NFC semifinals at Soldier Field. Fat chance.

Sean Landeta whiffed on a punt when a gust of wind blew the ball off his foot in the first quarter, and Shaun Gayle ran it in for a bizarre five-yard touchdown. Then Jim McMahon threw two third-quarter touchdown passes to Dennis McKinnon, and the Bears won comfortably 21–0.

But the story of the game—the story of the season—was the Bears' defense, as cold-hearted as the weather that chilled 62,076 delighted spectators. The Giants went three-and-out on nine of their first 11 possessions. Running back Joe Morris managed just 32 yards on 12 carries, 14 of those yards on his first attempt. Phil Simms was sacked six times. Before piling up 129 yards on their final two garbage-time drives, the Giants averaged less than two yards per play, and they were 0-for-12 on third-down conversions.

Buddy Ryan had promised a shutout, and his players delivered.

"We believe every thought Buddy shares with us," safety Dave Duerson said.

Defensive tackle William Perry set the tone, nailing Morris behind the line with a brutal hit that forced the 5-foot-7-inch running back from the game for a time with a mild concussion. "I got him with everything I had," Perry said.

The Giants came into the game with the No. 2-ranked defense in the NFL but left knowing the chasm separating them from the Bears was substantial. "Our defense—you've got to love them," coach Mike Ditka said. "Buddy did a great job coaching them."

Richard Dent led that defense with six tackles

With Jay Hilgenberg leading the interference, Walter Payton picks up some of his 93 yards against the Giants.

and 3 ¹/₂ sacks, spending the entire afternoon in Simms' face.

"They didn't know who to block," linebacker Wilber Marshall said. "That's what makes this defense so exciting. It's so complicated nobody can figure it out." Gayle became the ninth Bears defender to score this season with "my first touchdown since high school."

Meanwhile, the offensive line did not allow a sack to a Giants pass rush that led the league in sacks, completely neutralizing All-Pro linebacker Lawrence Taylor, who spent most of the fourth quarter on the sideline screaming in frustration.

McKinnon, who had three catches for 52 yards, first roused Taylor's ire with a devastating but legal crackback block on a first-quarter running play. He later mixed it up with Giants cornerback Elvis Patterson, whom he beat for both his touchdown catches.

"They call him Toast because he gets burned so often, right?" McKinnon said. "I didn't have toast for breakfast, but I had it for dinner."

The Bears' offense had no penalties or turnovers. With Walter Payton running for 93 yards, the Bears amassed 363 yards, which was 93 more than the Giants had been allowing.

"It wasn't easy," Ditka said. "Nothing in life is easy, but our players were on a mission. We beat a good football team."

No, they completely manhandled a good football team. What does that say about the Bears? ■

Chicago 21, New York 0
JAN. 5, 1986, AT SOLDIER FIELD

BOTTOM LINE
Stout defense as nasty as weather in demolition of Giants

KEY PLAY
After Sean Landeta whiffed on a first-quarter punt, Shaun Gayle's five-yard return gave the Bears a 7–0 lead that was more than enough.

KEY STAT
The Giants went three-and-out on nine of their first 11 possessions and were 0-for-12 on third-down conversions.

After Sean Landeta's phantom punt results in a five-yard touchdown for Shaun Gayle (23) in the NFC semifinal, Bears players and fans go wild (above). Mike Singletary closes in on New York's Phil Simms, who was sacked six times (right).

KEVIN BUTLER

No. 6, kicker

"Steve Kazor picked me up at the airport and we walked up to Halas Hall, and the first guy that walked up to me was Buddy Ryan. He goes, 'Hey, Steve, who's this?' Steve says, 'This is Kevin Butler.' Buddy looked at me and said, 'Oh, God, we wasted a pick on him.' All of a sudden I get a hand on my shoulder, and it was Ditka. Mike's like, 'Hey, don't listen to this guy. Come with me.'"

"If you didn't know where you stood with Mike, all you had to do was read the paper."

———————

"I remember my first meeting and sitting next to Mike Hartenstine and thinking, this guy's probably killed people. He had that demeanor—stone face. As I got to know Mike, there probably wasn't a nicer guy on the team."

———————

"The first mini-camp, I go up there after I'm drafted. I'm engaged to be married January 25. I walk out of that meeting, I get on the phone to Cathy and I say, 'Hey, we've got to change our wedding.' She's like, 'My God, you've been up there four hours and you've already met somebody.' I'm like, 'No, I'm going to make the team and we're going to the Super Bowl.'"

———————

"First of all, I hear 'Butthead.' That's my name for the rest of my life. I enjoy it. Every day in the mail, I'm still signing football cards."

———————

"Bear fans, they're true and blue. They've been through some lean years in the past. Until they carry the Lombardi Trophy off, we'll still be their favorite kids."

———————

The first thing that comes to my mind: I did contribute to that Super Bowl season. Two games: San Francisco and the New York Jets. I hit four field goals in each game. The Jets was a tighter game than the Frisco game, but the Frisco game

was a big game for me because the year before, that's where the Bears' season came to a halt in the NFC Championship Game. It was a big hump for us. To go out there and to make four field goals and to contribute to the win gave my teammates a lot of confidence in me."

"You get into the first playoff game that year, and it's the famous Sean Landeta missed punt. I'm thanking the Lord Landeta missed then because people forget I missed three that game."

"I made three in the Super Bowl. That was big momentum for us."

"The one thing the guys dug about me is that in 11 years, I never had a kickoff returned on me. I would get grief sometimes that I wasn't kicking the ball out of the end zone the way I did in college. If the other 10 guys aren't making the tackle, well, I'm going to make it. One year I was second in special-teams tackles with 11 solos."

"I've got a Super Bowl ring and trophy I love that's a great showpiece, and they can never take it away. But what football gave to me and Cathy, and what the Bears gave to me, is a tremendous head start in life. Hey, give me my health and give me my family, and I can get through anything." ∎

Chicago 24, Los Angeles 0
Super Smooth Sailing

Buddy Ryan had so much confidence in the Bears' impregnable, take-no-prisoners defense that he predicted three fumbles by Rams All-Pro running back Eric Dickerson in the NFC Championship Game. Ryan was wrong. Dickerson fumbled just twice. "If they would have run him more," Ryan scoffed, "he would have had three."

When Bear weather—frigid temperatures, howling winds, and swirling snow flurries—descended on Soldier Field, the Bears knew their first Super Bowl ticket was pretty well punched. In those conditions, Dickerson was the Southern California visitors' only hope. And he couldn't deliver, managing just 46 yards on 17 carries.

Worse, by falling behind 10–0 in the first 10 minutes and 34 seconds, the Rams were forced to play catch-up, and they had no chance against a defense that seemed to know what they were going to do before they even tried it and responded with

ferocious effectiveness in a 24–0 thumping. Overwhelmed quarterback Dieter Brock completed just 10 of 31 passes for 66 yards with one interception. He was sacked three times and spent the entire afternoon running for his life.

When did the Bears seize control? "Kickoff," said Dan Hampton, centerpiece of the defensive line that thwarted Dickerson and intimidated Brock. Early on, Hampton could see defeat in the Rams' faces. "I can tell by looking in their eyes whether they want to play or not," he said. "I knew they weren't really sure they wanted to be in Chicago playing us."

The Bears, who became the first team in NFL history to record back-to-back shutouts in the playoffs, were just as efficient if not as spectacular on offense, most notably Jim McMahon.

The punky QB completed 16 of 25 throws for 164 yards, running for one touchdown when he

Offensive guard Mark Bortz blocks the Rams' Gary Jeter as Jim McMahon prepares to pass.

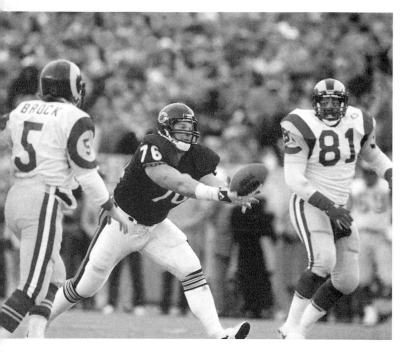

McMahon converted Dickerson's second fumble into a 22-yard TD pass to Willie Gault in the third quarter, waving off the draw play Ditka had sent in from the sidelines.

The defense got into the offensive act in the fourth quarter, Wilber Marshall returning Brock's fumble 52 yards for the game's final score after Brock had been dumped for the third time.

How one-sided was it? The Rams' longest drive was 27 yards. They went three-and-out on eight of their 16 possessions and averaged just 2.2 yards per play.

"I don't want to sound like I'm not happy about what happened today," Ditka said. "But we're on a mission, and it won't be finished until we're finished in New Orleans." ■

was supposed to pass and passing for another touchdown when he was supposed to hand off. He threw against the wind and with the wind and through the wind in a performance that drew superlatives from hard-to-please coach Mike Ditka.

"You don't understand how well our quarterback threw the football," Ditka said. McMahon's favorite target was Walter Payton, who gained only 32 yards rushing but added 48 yards on seven receptions.

After the Rams went three-and-out on their first possession, McMahon took the Bears 56 yards in five plays for a 7-0 lead, scoring the touchdown on a 16-yard run. Kevin Butler added a 34-yard field goal before the first quarter ended, and the tone of the day was set.

Chicago 24, Los Angeles 0
JAN. 12, 1986, AT SOLDIER FIELD

BOTTOM LINE
Defense, cold send Bears on way to New Orleans

KEY PLAY
Willie Gault's 22-yard touchdown reception. Jim McMahon waved off Mike Ditka's call for a draw play and hit Gault, who had faked cornerback LeRoy Irvin inside and then run a corner route.

KEY STAT
The Rams' longest drive covered 27 yards. They averaged 2.2 yards per play.

Among the hallmarks of the Bears' run to the NFC championship was the rugged defense of linemen Steve McMichael (above). Wilber Marshall steams into the end zone in the fourth quarter after scooping up a fumble (right).

BUDDY RYAN
Defensive coordinator

"In the meeting with defensive players the night before the Super Bowl I told them regardless of what happened, they'd always be my heroes, and walked out. They all were crying and yelling. It was a very emotional thing. I never planned much of anything like that. I found it works better if you have the feeling, you know?"

———

"Being carried off the field in the Super Bowl in New Orleans. That's a great honor that your players carried you off after the game. It's never been done to an assistant coach before or since."

———

"I don't have anything to tell you about Mike Ditka. I don't have feelings either way."

———

"Mr. Halas gave me the job a month before he hired Ditka and told me to hire my coaches."

———

"A dumb player gets you beat, and a guy that's scared will get you beat. You have to have intelligence and toughness. The players executed, and they just scared people. I think there was actually some fear. People laugh when you say 'NFL' and have somebody scared. Well, believe me, we had them scared."

"When they started out as rooks, they were numbers. As they got up and played well, I started calling them by name."

———

"If you remember, Mike Singletary and Todd Bell and Al Harris all held out that year. I spent the whole off-season begging them to sign up. Singletary did, but the other two didn't come into the fold, so they didn't get a Super Bowl ring."

———

"Moments that year? Oh, they were all great. Dominated in the Super Bowl the way we did."

———

"We'd always score the first 10 points of the game on defense and then give the offense the ball on the plus-40."

———

"Dan Hampton and I own some horses together, and he's kind of a country guy. Great player."

———

"If something broke down, Gary Fencik would jump the pattern. He's a super-smart guy. To play our defense, you had to be smart, and you had to be tough. Gary qualified both ways."

"They wanted me to play a three-man line, so they went out and got a nose tackle [William Perry], so they thought. But he could only play a couple plays, and then he had to rest."

"I used to play the players in racquetball in Chicago all the time. I competed that way. I beat them most of the time. McMahon could beat me. He's too good for me. But most of them I could beat."

"Weeb Ewbank hired me as an assistant coach for the New York Jets, and we only had four coaches back in those days, so you had to do it all—you had to draft, you had to scout, you had to coach. You learned a lot under Weeb."

"Joe Namath was a great player. He was a leader. He was the one who made it happen. Wore his white shoes."

"I had four brothers and two sisters. We were poor, but we didn't know it. We had clean clothes to wear and always had food on the table. We had great togetherness, really."

"I worked digging ditches and building roads, all kinds of things, anything that paid."

"I had a bunch of tough players over the years. Wilber Marshall was a tough guy. Otis Wilson was a tough guy. Gerry Philbin was a tough guy with the Jets. Then I had Alan Page and Carl Eller and Jim Marshall. Jerome Brown was a super-tough guy. I told you before, we looked for brains and toughness. Dumb guys get you beat, and cowards get you beat."

"I don't think there's anything misunderstood. You pretty well get what you see, don't you?" ■

Super Bowl XX

Chicago 46, New England 10
Mercy!

The Bears were far and away the most dominant team in football in 1985, so it was only appropriate that they wrapped up a storybook season with the most dominant performance in Super Bowl history. After taking Bourbon Street by storm during a week of frenzied buildup, they turned their attention to football and pulverized the New England Patriots 46–10 at the New Orleans Superdome. The game was so one-sided it evoked comparisons with an earlier Bears team's 73–0 destruction of the Washington Redskins in the 1940 NFL title game, football's previous standard for utter annihilation.

"Right now I'm so happy I could jump up to the top of the Superdome," All-Pro linebacker Mike Singletary said after orchestrating a defensive effort that drove New England quarterback Tony Eason from the game after six feeble possessions.

The Patriots actually scored first, converting a fumble into a field goal after Jim McMahon and Walter Payton missed connections on a handoff. The short-lived 3–0 lead deprived the Bears of an opportunity for a third straight postseason shutout. But by the time backup QB Steve Grogan got the Pats on the board again, it was 44–3. Grogan was then sacked for a fourth-quarter safety, making the 46–10 final score especially poignant because it was the "46" defense the Bears used to lay waste to the NFL all season.

"The game was never in question," coach Mike Ditka said.

Ditka, the star tight end on the Bears' last championship team in 1963, joined the Raiders' Tom Flores as the only men to play for and coach a Super Bowl champion. Ditka said he'd cherish this ring more, while remaining in debt to franchise founder George S. Halas, the late Papa Bear, who coached the '63 champions and who

William Perry dives for a one-yard touchdown that added controversy to Super Bowl XX.

gave Ditka the chance to coach the Bears.

"What you do in life by yourself doesn't mean as much as what you accomplish with a group of people," Ditka said. "It's because of Mr. Halas that I'm here. I'm just trying to pay some dues."

McMahon, whose antics in the week leading up to the game left him a marked man, responded with the sort of insouciant effectiveness that characterized his play all season. He completed 12 of 20 passes for 256 yards, setting up his own two touchdown runs and a third by Matt Suhey. "We could have got to 60 points, but we ran out of time," McMahon said. "And I would like to have seen a goose egg up there for them."

Willie Gault caught four passes for 129 yards, and charismatic 308-pound rookie William Perry bulldozed through the dazed Pats for his fourth touchdown of the season in the third quarter. That score, though, ignited the game's biggest controversy. Walter Payton, the proud face of the Bears franchise in some of its bleakest years, was denied an opportunity to score a Super Bowl touchdown.

Cornerback Reggie Phillips charges in with a 28-yard interception for a touchdown.

Payton led the Bears with 61 yards on 22 carries but failed to score.

"I wanted to get Walter into the end zone," Ditka insisted. "But our plays are designed to score, and I didn't know who had the ball."

"I feel very sad for No. 34," McMahon said.

Hurt feelings aside, it's a safe bet the Bears could have won without Payton and McMahon, so superior was their defense. They held the AFC champions to 123 total yards and 12 first downs, none in the first 25 minutes.

The defense also contributed to the point barrage when rookie cornerback Reggie Phillips returned a third-quarter interception 28 yards for a touchdown. Defensive end Richard Dent, leader of the pass rush that sent Eason scurrying for cover, was voted the Super Bowl's Most Valuable Player, but the Bears would have been just as happy if the award had gone to Buddy Ryan, architect of their fearsome defense.

"Buddy is the MVP of our defense," Singletary said. "He's a step ahead of everybody else. If it wasn't for him, what happened today wouldn't have happened. He's a real genius."

Singletary and his cohorts showed their appreciation at the final gun. As Ditka was being carried off the field, several defensive players hoisted Ryan to their shoulders and accorded him a similar tribute.

"I can't tell you how I feel about these guys," Ryan said. "They started off terrible this year. They gave up 28 points in the first game and were ranked 25th in the league. But they kept working like dogs to get it done. They did everything they could to be No. 1. That's what makes me so proud of these kids.

"This is the best defense that I've ever been with, and I've been with some awful good ones." ■

Chicago 46, New England 10
JAN. 26, 1986, AT THE SUPERDOME

BOTTOM LINE
46 points, '46' defense add up to utter domination

KEY PLAY
William Perry's third-quarter touchdown. Some of the Bears never forgave Mike Ditka for calling the Fridge's number instead of Walter Payton's from the 1-yard line.

KEY STAT
46–10. Total domination.

Afterword

After finishing my last reading of this book, I shut down my laptop, leaned back in my chair, stretched these creaky knees, and reflected on the Super Bowl Bears. Ah, yes, what a time it was. The magic came and left so quickly it seems maybe it never was here. But it was. Wasn't it?

Take my own roof. In 1986, six months after Super Bowl XX, workmen were doing some repairs up there—seems somebody was always hammering above—and I had a brainstorm: what if I put a sign there? The roof itself was very steep, too steep to stand on, but a worker had a roof ladder, the kind of ladder that has a piece that hooks over the peak and lays flat against the shingles. Before dusk I got a bucket of white house paint and a brush from the garage, climbed a regular ladder to the roof, clambered onto the roof ladder and sat there, looking out at the deserted Bears practice field and Halas Hall.

From the players' vantage point, my black roof would be a billboard staring them in the face, a "SEE ROCK CITY" barn along a Tennessee highway. I carefully pried off the lid of the gallon can and began to paint. I was bubbling with Super Bowl giddiness, like all Bears fans, and this is what I painted: "46–10."

I didn't hear much from folks for a while— you had to be on the field to really notice, but from there it was like a neon sign in your eyeballs—until a year later Ditka saw me at a practice and said, "Could you get that damn score off your roof? We haven't done crap."

He was mad because the Bears had lost the 1986 NFC playoff game to the Washington Redskins, and the Super Bowl score was a sharp stick in his side. It took a while, but I located the roof ladder again, maybe I called the worker who owned it, and I went back up on the roof. I painted a line through the 46–10 and painted, directly above it: "13–27," the losing score of that Redskins playoff game. Another year went by, and the Bears lost in the playoffs again. To the Redskins.

"Dammit!" Ditka said this time. "Get those scores off your roof! They're killing me!"

But here was the problem. The roof ladder was gone, the workmen were long gone, and I wasn't interested in climbing onto those black shingles

248

again, by any means. I could see myself tumbling off, being impaled on the fence below, ending a brief career with a bad obituary headline.

"Coach, I'm sorry, I can't get up there," I said. "But you can do whatever you want."

Time went by. One day I heard a whirring noise, a bump on the roof. I went onto my deck. The Bears' cherry-picker, the cranelike contraption from which cameraman Mitch Friedman filmed practice, had been driven to the edge of Bears territory, tilted forward, and now somebody was leaning out, painting my roof with a long roller and black paint. The score was gone.

After a few years the numerals started to creep out. Then, in 1993, Lake Forest was hit by a bad hailstorm, and the insurance company replaced my entire roof. In 1997 the Bears moved to new Halas Hall in another part of town, and that was that.

What remains are the memories, the former players, and the coach—Ditka. If that 1985 season had all of the elements of the mythological journey—the leader with an outsized goal, the band of characters, the trek, the battles, the temporary failure (Miami), the wise old adviser (Landry), the internal strife (Buddy), the redemption, the goal achieved, the uncertainty after success—Ditka has become the embodiment of the adventure. He could have become a clown, a caricature, even a

nobody. But he stayed in the public eye, being wise, being funny, being angry, being absurd, making contradictions, doing such things as saying he's running for U.S. senator, making a movie, appearing on radio and TV, selling an erectile dysfunction drug, even coaching the woeful New Orleans Saints for a spell. "It's funny," he told me of that miscalculation, "but the Bears played our Super Bowl in New Orleans, and because of that I thought somehow I could make it Chicago down there." Ricky Williams was going to be Ditka's new Walter Payton. Wrong.

Now people genuinely like old No. 89. Maybe love isn't too strong a word. His V-hairdo and mustache are not just trademarks, they're fun, they're legend. Folks revere Ditka because he personifies things seemingly lost—guy-dom, the era before political correctness, old-time nasty football. But they also revere him because they can tell somewhere inside that huge, snarling carcass is a soft touch, a great big beating heart. In fact, more and more that kindness is right on the surface.

"I eat quitters for breakfast and spit out the bones!" Ditka bellows in Kicking and Screaming. But he's winking the whole time.

Of course, he twitches with unfulfilled want. It's as though he's the biggest toddler in the world. It's like he was built with attack mode only and a dial that goes to 12. He fidgets, he plays solitaire, he grumbles to himself, he plays golf in the wind, snow, sleet. Sharks rest more than he does, even at age 70. You look at Iron Mike, and you know what he should be doing forever is catching a pass across the short middle, seeking a collision with the tough-guy linebackers and maybe a couple safeties, if they want some.

It was fitting that we spent so much time in his cigar bar over the years. "If people don't like smoke, they don't have to come," he'd say, firing up a stogie. It's perfect, because public smoking is now as vanished as the dodo. I never saw a dodo, but I miss those birds.

I think of Ditka's comments about Grabowskis and Smiths. Doug Smith, the Los Angeles Rams Pro Bowl center in 1985, told me back then, "My name's been Smith all along, and I never associated it with white collar or conformity. I mean, they're the ones making videos. We could make a video and there would be 50 sales—to our families."

He was right. The Bears were all kinds of things. Ditka himself was the Grabowski. And part of a Grabowski's essence is being restless, always slightly teed-off, ever the self-perceived underdog. Ditka can make a comment, then later reverse himself, then crisscross it all like a foaming speed-boat. Confront him with the wavy contradictions, and he'll solve everything by spouting, "Well, you can kiss my ass!"

Diana Ditka has seen it all. "Mike is just so honest," she says. And honestly, aren't we all contradictions like Mike? Isn't that the appeal? No matter how deep-thinking we get, don't we invariably come back to the caveman principal regarding life's ambiguities: kick its ass before it kicks yours?

A while back, my son and two buddies were sitting at our kitchen table, watching an NFL game on TV. I said to them, apropos of nothing, "So the entire continent of Europe takes on 11 mini-Ditkas in a game of football. Who wins?"

"Easy, Mr. Telander," said one boy, still polite, even as a teenager. "The mini-Ditkas."

"By how much?"

"Two hundred thirty-seven to nothing."

"Correct," I said.

I recalled more Saturday Night Live "Super Fan" logic.

"Ditka and God are sitting at a bar," I said. "What are they talking about?"

"Trick question!" the boys shouted in unison.

"Why?" I asked.

"Ditka is God!"

Whatever he is, you gotta believe he's a treasure.

—*Rick Telander, July 2010*

GAME 1
SEPT. 8 at SOLDIER FIELD

38 BEARS | **28** BUCCANEERS

TAMPA BAY	14	14	0	0	28
BEARS	7	10	14	7	38

FIRST QUARTER

BUCS: Magee 1 pass from DeBerg (Igwebuike kick), 7:06.

BEARS: McKinnon 21 pass from McMahon (Butler kick), 12:11.

BUCS: House 44 pass from DeBerg (Igwebuike kick), 12:33.

SECOND QUARTER

BUCS: Bell 11 pass from DeBerg (Igwebuike kick), 3:29.

BEARS: McMahon 1 run (Butler kick), 6:51.

BEARS: Butler 38 FG, 12:25.

BUCS: Wilder 3 run (Igwebuike kick), 13:51.

THIRD QUARTER

BEARS: Frazier 29 interception return (Butler kick), :22.

BEARS: Suhey 9 pass from McMahon (Butler kick), 14:33.

FOURTH QUARTER

BEARS: McMahon 1 run (Butler kick), 2:28.

TEAM STATS	T.B.	CHI.
First downs	17	27
Total net yards	307	436
Rushes-yards	29-166	34-185
Passing yards	141	251
Return yards	21	55
Comp-att-int	13-21-2	23-34-1
Sacked-yards	2-19	3-23
Punts-avg	6-37	2-58
Fumbles-lost	0-0	2-2
Penalties-yards	12-80	8-78
Time of possession	26:41	33:19

GAME 2
SEPT. 15 at SOLDIER FIELD

20 BEARS | **7** PATRIOTS

NEW ENGLAND	0	0	0	7	7
BEARS	7	3	10	0	20

FIRST QUARTER

BEARS: McKinnon 32 pass from McMahon (Butler kick), 3:03.

SECOND QUARTER

BEARS: Butler 21 FG, 14:23.

THIRD QUARTER

BEARS: Suhey 1 run (Butler kick), 10:44.

BEARS: Butler 28 FG, 13:38.

FOURTH QUARTER

PATRIOTS: James 90 pass from Eason (Franklin kick), 5:57.

TEAM STATS	N.E.	CHI.
First downs	10	18
Total net yards	206	369
Rushes-yards	16-27	44-160
Passing yards	179	209
Return yards	116	157
Comp-att-int	15-35-3	13-23-1
Sacked-yards	6-55	3-23
Punts-avg	11-47	8-37
Fumbles-lost	1-1	1-1
Penalties-yards	8-70	2-10
Time of possession	22:35	37:25

GAME 3
SEPT. 19 at THE METRODOME

33 BEARS | **24** VIKINGS

BEARS	3	3	24	3	33
MINNESOTA	3	7	7	7	24

FIRST QUARTER

BEARS: Butler 24 FG, 8:36.

VIKINGS: Stenerud 25 FG, 14:49.

SECOND QUARTER

BEARS: Butler 19 FG, 11:35.

VIKINGS: Carter 14 pass from Kramer (Stenerud kick), 14:13.

THIRD QUARTER

BEARS: Butler 34 FG, 3:30.

VIKINGS: Jones 9 pass from Kramer (Stenerud kick), 7:28.

BEARS: Gault 70 pass from McMahon (Butler kick), 7:47.

BEARS: McKinnon 25 pass from McMahon (Butler kick), 9:35.

BEARS: McKinnon 43 pass from McMahon (Butler kick), 14:27.

FOURTH QUARTER

VIKINGS: Carter 57 pass from Kramer (Stenerud kick), 5:41.

BEARS: Butler 31 FG, 9:25.

TEAM STATS	CHI.	MINN.
First downs	21	23
Total net yards	480	445
Rushes-yards	30-127	15-34
Passing yards	353	411
Return yards	193	182
Comp-att-int	21-33-1	28-55-3
Sacked-yards	1-7	4-25
Punts-avg	3-40	3-43
Fumbles-lost	0-0	3-2
Penalties-yards	10-66	6-45
Time of possession	31:44	28:16

GAME 4
SEPT. 29 at SOLDIER FIELD

45 BEARS | **10** REDSKINS

WASHINGTON	7	3	0	0	10
BEARS	0	31	7	7	45

FIRST QUARTER

REDSKINS: Riggins 7 run (Moseley kick), 8:52.

SECOND QUARTER

REDSKINS: Moseley 32 FG, :06.

BEARS: Gault 99 kickoff return (Butler kick), :27.

BEARS: McKinnon 14 pass from McMahon (Butler kick), 2:33.

BEARS: Moorehead 10 pass from McMahon (Butler kick), 5:41.

BEARS: McMahon 13 pass from Payton (Butler kick), 10:33.

BEARS: Butler 28 FG, 14:56.

THIRD QUARTER

BEARS: Payton 33 pass from McMahon (Butler kick), 9:37.

FOURTH QUARTER

BEARS: Gentry 1 run (Butler kick), 9:33.

TEAM STATS	WASH.	CHI.
First downs	19	16
Total net yards	376	250
Rushes-yards	35-192	22-91
Passing yards	184	159
Return yards	182	217
Comp-att-int	21-39-2	14-21-1
Sacked-yards	4-25	3-14
Punts-avg	5-27	5-41
Fumbles-lost	1-1	0-0
Penalties-yards	10-85	6-50
Time of possession	34:25	25:35

GAME 5
OCT. 6 at TAMPA STADIUM

27 BEARS | **19** BUCCANEERS

BEARS	0	3	10	14	27
TAMPA BAY	0	12	0	7	19

SECOND QUARTER

BUCS: Igwebuike 19 FG, 4:04.

BUCS: House 21 pass from DeBerg (kick failed), 8:38.

BUCS: Igwebuike 36 FG, 13:09.

BEARS: Butler 30 FG, 14:59.

THIRD QUARTER

BEARS: McKinnon 21 pass from McMahon (Butler kick), 11:20.

BEARS: Butler 30 FG, 15:00.

FOURTH QUARTER

BEARS: Payton 4 run (Butler kick), 7:09.

BUCS: Carter 25 pass from DeBerg (Igwebuike kick), 9:39.

BEARS: Payton 9 run (Butler kick), 14:08.

TEAM STATS	CHI.	T.B.
First downs	22	19
Total net yards	433	373
Rushes-yards	32-147	20-27
Passing yards	286	346
Return yards	156	134
Comp-att-int	22-34-2	23-43-2
Sacked-yards	1-6	0-0
Punts-avg	4-54	4-45
Fumbles-lost	2-1	3-1
Penalties-yards	9-67	5-40
Time of possession	32:09	27:51

Appendix: 1985 Game Statistics

GAME 6
OCT. 13 at CANDLESTICK PARK

26 BEARS | **10 49ERS**

BEARS	13	3	0	10	26
SAN FRANCISCO	0	10	0	0	10

FIRST QUARTER
BEARS: Payton 3 run (Butler kick), 2:29.
BEARS: Butler 34 FG, 7:42.
BEARS: Butler 38 FG, 10:06.

SECOND QUARTER
BEARS: Butler 27 FG, 1:05.
49ERS: Williamson 43 interception return (Wersching kick), 6:03.
49ERS: Wersching 32 FG, 14:11.

FOURTH QUARTER
BEARS: Butler 29 FG, 1:51.
BEARS: Payton 17 run (Butler kick), 11:19.

TEAM STATS

	CHI.	S.F.
First downs	22	11
Total net yards	372	183
Rushes-yards	30-189	12-67
Passing yards	183	116
Return yards	101	218
Comp-att-int	18-31-1	17-29-0
Sacked-yards	1-3	7-44
Punts-avg	3-45	7-48
Fumbles-lost	1-0	4-2
Penalties-yards	7-45	13-04
Time of possession	36:37	23:23

GAME 7
OCT. 21 at SOLDIER FIELD

23 BEARS | **7 PACKERS**

GREEN BAY	7	0	0	0	7
BEARS	0	21	0	2	23

FIRST QUARTER
PACKERS: Lofton 27 pass from Dickey (Del Greco kick), 8:02.

SECOND QUARTER
BEARS: Payton 2 run (Butler kick), 1:19.
BEARS: Perry 1 run (Butler kick), 5:08.
BEARS: Payton 1 run (Butler kick), 13:49.

FOURTH QUARTER
BEARS: Safety, Wilson tackled Zorn in end zone, 10:59.

TEAM STATS

	G.B.	CHI.
First downs	16	24
Total net yards	319	342
Rushes-yards	26-96	41-175
Passing yards	223	167
Return yards	64	131
Comp-att-int	14-31-4	15-32-0
Sacked-yards	4-27	3-5
Punts-avg	6-40	5-55
Fumbles-lost	2-1	7-4
Penalties-yards	10-70	6-45
Time of possession	24:25	35:35

GAME 8
OCT. 27 at SOLDIER FIELD

27 BEARS | **9 VIKINGS**

MINNESOTA	0	7	0	2	9
BEARS	10	3	7	7	27

FIRST QUARTER
BEARS: McKinnon 33 pass from McMahon (Butler kick), 3:31.
BEARS: Butler 40 FG, 12:20.

SECOND QUARTER
VIKINGS: Nelson 1 run (Stenerud kick), :51.
BEARS: Butler 29 FG, 14:58.

THIRD QUARTER
BEARS: Wilson 23 interception return (Butler kick), 3:40.

FOURTH QUARTER
BEARS: Payton 20 pass from McMahon (Butler kick), 5:24.
VIKINGS: Safety, Elshire tackled Fuller in end zone, 7:15.

TEAM STATS

	MINN.	CHI.
First downs	16	24
Total net yards	236	413
Rushes-yards	14-30	39-202
Passing yards	206	211
Return yards	137	132
Comp-att-int	21-46-3	19-34-1
Sacked-yards	4-30	1-4
Punts-avg	6-42	4-47
Fumbles-lost	0-0	1-1
Penalties-yards	8-60	6-77
Time of possession	25:18	34:42

GAME 9
NOV. 3 at LAMBEAU FIELD

16 BEARS | **10 PACKERS**

BEARS	0	7	0	9	16
GREEN BAY	3	0	7	0	10

FIRST QUARTER
PACKERS: Del Greco 40 FG, 2:21.

SECOND QUARTER
BEARS: Perry 4 pass from McMahon (Butler kick), 14:35.

THIRD QUARTER
PACKERS: Clark 55 pass from Zorn (Del Greco kick), 9:45.

FOURTH QUARTER
BEARS: Safety, McMichael tackled Zorn in end zone, 2:42.
BEARS: Payton 27 run (Butler kick), 4:29.

TEAM STATS

	CHI.	G.B.
First downs	16	15
Total net yards	253	242
Rushes-yards	37-188	28-87
Passing yards	65	155
Return yards	112	70
Comp-att-int	9-20-0	11-26-1
Sacked-yards	3-26	3-24
Punts-avg	8-39	6-37
Fumbles-lost	1-1	2-0
Penalties-yards	7-70	8-66
Time of possession	30:57	29:03

GAME 10
NOV. 10 at SOLDIER FIELD

24 BEARS | **3 LIONS**

DETROIT	0	0	3	0	3
BEARS	7	7	7	3	24

FIRST QUARTER
BEARS: Fuller 1 run (Butler kick), 14:20.

SECOND QUARTER
BEARS: Thomas 7 run (Butler kick), 11:50.

THIRD QUARTER
LIONS: Murray 34 FG, 9:59.
BEARS: Fuller 5 run (Butler kick), 14:32.

FOURTH QUARTER
BEARS: Butler 39 FG, 9:18.

TEAM STATS

	DET.	CHI.
First downs	8	26
Total net yards	106	360
Rushes-yards	22-68	55-250
Passing yards	38	110
Return yards	80	35
Comp-att-int	8-17-2	7-13-0
Sacked-yards	4-35	1-2
Punts-avg	3-31	2-21
Fumbles-lost	3-2	3-2
Penalties-yards	6-31	5-40
Time of possession	18:58	41:02

GAME 11
NOV. 17 at TEXAS STADIUM

44 BEARS | **0** COWBOYS

BEARS	7	17	3	17	44
DALLAS	0	0	0	0	0

FIRST QUARTER

BEARS: Dent 1 interception return (Butler kick), 13:12.

SECOND QUARTER

BEARS: Butler 44 FG, 5:13.

BEARS: Richardson 36 interception return (Butler kick), 9:19.

BEARS: Fuller 1 run (Butler kick), 12:02.

THIRD QUARTER

BEARS: Butler 46 FG, 14:24.

FOURTH QUARTER

BEARS: Butler 22 FG, 3:02.

BEARS: Thomas 17 run (Butler kick), 7:13.

BEARS: Gentry 16 run (Butler kick), 12:22.

TEAM STATS

	CHI.	DAL.
First downs	18	12
Total net yards	378	171
Rushes-yards	40-216	16-52
Passing yards	162	119
Return yards	137	196
Comp-att-int	10-25-1	15-39-4
Sacked-yards	4-35	6-48
Punts-avg	6-44	10-38
Fumbles-lost	1-0	1-1
Penalties-yards	8-105	6-65
Time of possession	35:18	24:42

GAME 12
NOV. 24 at SOLDIER FIELD

36 BEARS | **0** FALCONS

ATLANTA	0	0	0	0	0
BEARS	0	20	7	9	36

SECOND QUARTER

BEARS: Butler 35 FG, :47.

BEARS: Butler 32 FG, 6:22.

BEARS: Payton 40 run (Butler kick), 8:52.

BEARS: Perry 1 run (Butler kick), 13:04.

THIRD QUARTER

BEARS: Thomas 2 run (Butler kick), 5:41.

FOURTH QUARTER

BEARS: Safety, Waechter tackled Holly in end zone, 1:46.

BEARS: Sanders 1 run (Butler kick), 11:25.

TEAM STATS

	ATL.	CHI.
First downs	10	24
Total net yards	119	379
Rushes-yards	37-141	43-196
Passing yards	(-22)	183
Return yards	105	112
Comp-att-int	3-17-2	12-24-0
Sacked-yards	5-38	1-1
Punts-avg	7-38	4-38
Fumbles-lost	1-1	1-1
Penalties-yards	9-82	5-45
Time of possession	27:08	32:52

GAME 13
DEC. 2 at THE ORANGE BOWL

38 DOLPHINS | **24** BEARS

BEARS	7	3	14	0	24
MIAMI	10	21	7	0	38

FIRST QUARTER

DOLPHINS: Moore 33 pass from Marino (Reveiz kick), 3:51.

BEARS: Fuller 1 run (Butler kick), 6:39.

DOLPHINS: Reveiz 47 FG, 9:04.

SECOND QUARTER

DOLPHINS: Davenport 1 run (Reveiz kick), :07.

BEARS: Butler 30 FG, 8:20.

DOLPHINS: Davenport 1 run (Reveiz kick), 13:03.

DOLPHINS: Moore 6 pass from Marino (Reveiz kick), 13:43.

THIRD QUARTER

BEARS: Fuller 1 run (Butler kick), 5:35.

DOLPHINS: Clayton 42 pass from Marino (Reveiz kick), 6:27.

BEARS: Margerum 19 pass from Fuller (Butler kick), 8:35.

TEAM STATS

	CHI.	MIA.
First downs	23	17
Total net yards	343	335
Rushes-yards	37-167	24-90
Passing yards	176	245
Return yards	153	101
Comp-att-int	14-28-3	14-27-1
Sacked-yards	6-35	3-25
Punts-avg	3-29	3-45
Fumbles-lost	1-1	2-1
Penalties-yards	7-65	6-61
Time of possession	34:08	25:52

GAME 14
DEC. 8 at SOLDIER FIELD

17 BEARS | **10** COLTS

INDIANAPOLIS	0	3	0	7	10
BEARS	0	3	7	7	17

SECOND QUARTER

BEARS: Butler 20 FG, 3:57.

COLTS: Allegre 30 FG, 9:26.

THIRD QUARTER

BEARS: Payton 16 run (Butler kick), 13:07.

FOURTH QUARTER

BEARS: Thomas 3 run (Butler kick), 8:51.

Colts: Capers 61 pass from Pagel (Allegre kick), 9:03.

COLTS: Capers 61 pass from Pagel (Allegre kick), 9:03.

Colts: Capers 61 pass from Pagel (Allegre kick), 9:03.

TEAM STATS

	IND.	CHI.
First downs	10	22
Total net yards	232	328
Rushes-yards	21-99	44-191
Passing yards	133	137
Return yards	117	93
Comp-att-int	10-24-0	11-23-0
Sacked-yards	1-10	3-8
Punts-avg	4-50	4-44
Fumbles-lost	0-0	0-0
Penalties-yards	3-25	5-45
Time of possession	21:05	38:55

GAME 15
DEC. 14 at GIANTS STADIUM

19 BEARS | **6** JETS

BEARS	3	7	3	6	19
NEW YORK	3	0	3	0	6

FIRST QUARTER

BEARS: Butler 18 FG, 10:55.

JETS: Leahy 23 FG, 13:19.

SECOND QUARTER

BEARS: Wrightman 7 pass from McMahon (Butler kick), 4:02.

THIRD QUARTER

JETS: Leahy 55 FG, 1:57.

BEARS: Butler 31 FG, 4:06.

FOURTH QUARTER

BEARS: Butler 36 FG, 11:19.

Bears: Butler 21 FG, 14:43.

BEARS: Butler 21 FG, 14:43.

Bears: Butler 21 FG, 14:43.

TEAM STATS

	CHI.	N.Y.
First downs	20	11
Total net yards	319	159
Rushes-yards	40-116	23-70
Passing yards	203	89
Return yards	36	106
Comp-att-int	15-31-1	12-26-0
Sacked-yards	5-12	4-33
Punts-avg	7-36	6-37
Fumbles-lost	1-0	3-3
Penalties-yards	5-46	5-45
Time of possession	39:36	20:24

GAME 16
DEC. 22 at PONTIAC SILVERDOME

37 BEARS | **17** LIONS

BEARS	3	3	10	21	**37**
DETROIT	3	0	7	7	**17**

FIRST QUARTER
BEARS: Butler 25 FG, 5:40.
LIONS: Murray 42 FG, 14:41.

SECOND QUARTER
BEARS: Butler 24 FG, 13:03.

THIRD QUARTER
BEARS: Gentry 94 kickoff return (Butler kick), :20.
BEARS: Butler 21 FG, 10:33.
LIONS: Lewis 2 pass from Hipple (Murray kick), 13:32.

FOURTH QUARTER
BEARS: McMahon 14 run (Butler kick), 1:16.
BEARS: Rivera 5 fumble recovery return (Butler kick), 1:44.
LIONS: Jones 2 run (Murray kick), 3:59.
BEARS: Margerum 11 pass from McMahon (Butler kick), 13:00.

TEAM STATS	CHI.	DET.
First downs	20	22
Total net yards	382	326
Rushes-yards	33-161	21-73
Passing yards	221	253
Return yards	282	202
Comp-att-int	14-26-3	24-47-3
Sacked-yards	4-23	6-45
Punts-avg	1-40	3-41
Fumbles-lost	2-1	4-4
Penalties-yards	8-58	2-15
Time of possession	33:00	27:00

GAME 17 • NFC SEMIFINAL GAME
JAN. 5 at SOLDIER FIELD

 21 BEARS | **0** GIANTS

NEW YORK	0	0	0	0	**0**
BEARS	7	0	14	0	**21**

FIRST QUARTER
BEARS: Gayle 5 punt return (Butler kick), 9:32.

THIRD QUARTER
BEARS: McKinnon 23 pass from McMahon (Butler kick), 6:12.
BEARS: McKinnon 20 pass from McMahon (Butler kick), 14:23.

TEAM STATS	N.Y.	CHI.
First downs	10	17
Total net yards	181	363
Rushes-yards	14-32	44-147
Passing yards	149	216
Return yards	104	48
Comp-att-int	14-35-0	11-21-0
Sacked-yards	6-60	0-0
Punts-avg	9-38	6-37
Fumbles-lost	3-1	0-0
Penalties-yards	4-25	2-20
Time of possession	22:46	37:14

GAME 18 • NFC CHAMPIONSHIP GAME
JAN. 12 at SOLDIER FIELD

 24 BEARS | **0** RAMS

LOS ANGELES	0	0	0	0	**0**
BEARS	10	0	7	7	**24**

FIRST QUARTER
BEARS: McMahon 16 run (Butler kick), 5:25.
BEARS: Butler 34 FG, 10:34.

THIRD QUARTER
BEARS: Gault 22 pass from McMahon (Butler kick), 8:04.

FOURTH QUARTER
BEARS: Marshall 52 fumble recovery return (Butler kick), 12:23.

TEAM STATS	L.A.	CHI.
First downs	13	9
Total net yards	130	232
Rushes-yards	26-86	33-91
Passing yards	44	141
Return yards	92	40
Comp-att-int	10-31-1	16-25-0
Sacked-yards	3-22	3-23
Punts-avg	11-39	10-36
Fumbles-lost	4-2	3-1
Penalties-yards	4-25	6-48
Time of possession	25:33	34:27

GAME 19 • SUPER BOWL XX
JAN. 26 at NEW ORLEANS SUPERDOME

 46
BEARS

10
PATRIOTS

BEARS	13	10	21	2	**46**
NEW ENGLAND	3	0	0	7	**10**

FIRST QUARTER

PATRIOTS: Franklin 36 FG, 1:19.
Drive: 4 plays, 0 yards.
Key play: McGrew recovery of Payton fumble at Bears' 19.

BEARS: Butler 28 FG, 5:40.
Drive: 8 plays, 59 yards.
Key play: Gault 43 pass from McMahon.

BEARS: Butler 24 FG, 13:39.
Drive: 7 plays, 7 yards.
Key play: Hampton recovery of Eason fumble at New England 13.

BEARS: Suhey 11 run (Butler kick), 14:37.
Drive: 2 plays, 13 yards.
Key play: Singletary recovery of James fumble at New England 13.

SECOND QUARTER

BEARS: McMahon 2 run (Butler kick), 7:36.
Drive: 10 plays, 59 yards.
Key play: Suhey 24 pass from McMahon.

BEARS: Butler 25 FG, 15:00.
Drive: 11 plays, 72 yards.
Key play: Margerum 29 pass from McMahon.

THIRD QUARTER

BEARS: McMahon 1 run (Butler kick), 7:38.
Drive: 9 plays, 96 yards.
Key play: Gault 60 pass from McMahon.

BEARS: Phillips 28 interception return (Butler kick), 8:44.

BEARS: Perry 1 run (Butler kick), 11:38.
Drive: 6 plays, 37 yards.
Key play: Marshall recovery of James fumble at 50, returned by Marshall and Wilson to 37.

FOURTH QUARTER

PATRIOTS: Fryar 8 pass from Grogan (Franklin kick), 1:46.
Drive: 15 plays, 76 yards.
Key play: Morgan 21 pass from Grogan.

BEARS: Safety, Waechter tackled Grogan in end zone, 9:24.

TEAM STATS	CHI.	N.E.
First downs	23	12
By rushing	13	1
By passing	9	10
By penalty	1	1
Third-down conversions	7-14	1-10
Offensive plays	76	54
Total net yards	408	123
Yards per play	5.4	2.3
Rushes-yards	49-167	11-7
Gain per rush	3.4	0.6
Passing yards	241	116
Comp-att-int	12-24-0	17-36-2
Gain per pass	10.0	3.2

TEAM STATS	CHI.	N.E.
Sacked-yards	3-15	7-61
Return yards	144	175
Punt return yards	2-20	2-22
Kickoff return yards	4-49	7-153
Interceptions	2-75	0-0
Fumbles-lost	3-2	4-4
Punts-avg	4-43	6-44
Penalties-yards	6-35	5-35
Touchdowns	5	1
By rushing	4	0
By passing	0	1
By returns	1	0
Field goals	3-3	1-1